This
Life
Is
Yours

This
Life
Is
Yours

DISCOVER YOUR POWER, CLAIM YOUR
WHOLENESS, AND HEAL YOUR LIFE

Linda Martella-Whitsett and Alicia Whitsett

HAMPTON ROADS

Cover design by Kathryn Sky-Peck
Cover photograph by portishead1/Getty Images
Interior by Deborah Dutton
Typeset in Weiss and Avenir LT

Hampton Roads Publishing Company, Inc.
Charlottesville, VA 22906
Distributed by Red Wheel/Weiser, LLC
www.redwheelweiser.com

Sign up for our newsletter and special offers by going to
www.redwheelweiser.com/newsletter.

ISBN: 978-1-64297-013-5

Library of Congress Cataloging-in-Publication Data available upon
request.

Printed in Canada
MAR
10 9 8 7 6 5 4 3 2 1

We dedicate this book to many beautiful beings we have met who courageously claim wholeness in the face of challenging conditions. Your stories have encouraged us and empowered us to share our own.

CONTENTS

INTRODUCTION

This is a book about healing yourself rather than curing a condition. Through healing, you can recover your whole *self*, your enlightened *self*—which is greater than anything you could imagine to be missing, wrong, or broken about you. We view healing as an intentional, continual self-directed practice that reconciles your fully human and fully spiritual natures. We believe *you* can heal yourself, no matter the circumstances.

You can begin by following this advice: Pause rather than rolling headlong in pursuit of a cure or your desired outcome. It is our experience that scrambling to find a solution—any solution—propels you out ahead of yourself, in a sense, leaving yourself behind. We have learned that healing happens right where you are, on the inside, and that healing your life rather than your conditions is key to all that you truly desire. Your aim must be to become conscious about your life, to question your assumptions and beliefs, and to mine the rich ore of wisdom within as a guide for your next choices.

In this book, we address common questions about healing, some of which may be on your mind. Among these are:

- When I long for healing with a particular outcome in mind, how can I say it was successful if I do not achieve that outcome?

- Is it really healing if it's not just as I desired it to be?

- Is there a trick to healing—a formula, a particular set of steps?

- Why is this happening to me? What caused it to happen and how long will the healing take?

- If I pray every day for healing without results, am I praying in the wrong way? Is there a right way to pray for healing?

- Is it worse to hope for a miracle than just to manage day by day? Isn't hoping futile?

　　　　　　　　　　　　This Life Is Yours

- When time passes without my seeing the desired outcome, does it mean, as people say, that "there must be something better in store"?

- How can I be whole or complete and not feel it?

- If healing is in my hands, how can I increase my power to heal?

Throughout this book, we promise we will not tell you what we think you need to do. We believe the direction you take in healing is unique to you and that you have within you the wisdom and strength to determine what will be best for you. We hope, rather, to share many perspectives and possibilities, some of which you may not have contemplated before.

We will explore many spiritual principles that are unrelated to particular faith traditions. Our own tradition, the Unity Movement, was founded in metaphysical Christianity and teaches about our oneness with the divine. Spiritual practices like prayer and meditation are the tools we use to harness the power of our minds and transform our experience, pivoting awareness away from our concerns and toward our inner strengths. We refer to this capacity as the law of mind action, more commonly known nowadays as the "law of attraction."

We encourage you to integrate our message into your own religious practices. Whether you have faith in a deity, subscribe to a higher power, or believe in the power of the human spirit, we offer our message as one that you can integrate into your understanding.

We are not medical professionals and we will not discuss or prescribe medical protocols. We will, however, recommend practices for bodily, mental, and spiritual well-being. We encourage you to discuss any insights you derive from your reading with your medical providers to see if they could impact your medical care.

We each direct our own healing and tell our own story. Your story may be anchored in whatever you believe is missing, wrong, or broken in your life. Or it may be elevated by your newfound courage, evolving understanding, and conscious choices. This is what excited us as we contemplated writing this book. As a mother and daughter—each on our own life path, each with our own story—we recognize in each other certain strengths that we believe can inspire readers. We also acknowledge that many of our stories stem from shared experiences. We strive to behold each other's wholeness, while allowing ourselves to be where we are in our own discoveries without interference.

We wrote this book to respect you and where you are in your own experience, as well as to support you as you learn to direct your own healing. Our hope is that it will help you reflect on the unique meaning of wholeness and healing in your life, and examine any current beliefs and perspectives that may be impacting your healing. Our

This Life Is Yours

goal is to help you select intentional actions that will help you heal and reclaim your wholeness.

We encourage you to use this book as a reference for the choices you make each day. We hope you will refer to it for encouragement and consult it as a source of relevant affirmations and recommended practices as they inspire you.

So here's to the whole you! Here's to who you thought you were. And here's to where you are right in this moment. It is time for you to claim your wholeness.

CHAPTER 1

From Healing to Wholeness

Through the oneness that lives inside of you, me, and all humans who walk the planet, we have a direct line to the same force that creates everything from atoms and stars to the DNA of life.

—Gregg Braden, *The Divine Matrix*

Everyone knows someone—or is someone—who is working through an illness, a loss, or a challenging life circumstance. In times like these, wholeness and healing become prevalent themes. Wholeness is often understood as a destination, while healing is often seen as a method to get from an unwanted condition to a desired goal. The presumption is that wholeness is something to be achieved, while healing is something you do to achieve it. In this chapter, we offer empowering perspectives on wholeness and healing as a framework for self-discovery and self-mastery.

WHOLENESS

Wholeness is the original and absolute "you"—the "you" that, in any moment, can know itself and feel itself. The "you" that is, in any moment, an integration of all that has ever been. The "you" that is complete, in that nothing about you can be missing or unfinished in this moment. The "you" that is a complex system of relationships that cannot exist without one another. The "you" that is ever-evolving pure potential and infinite possibility.

We can know wholeness as the integration of body, mind, and spirit, the building blocks of our humanity. But we also can recognize that we are more than just human. We are spiritual beings. Wholeness means that we are both human and divine.

Wholeness is the original and absolute you. It reaches beyond you, encompassing you, fueling you. The wholeness that you are exists within the whole—all of it, all of everything. It's the web of connectivity, the field of infinite intelligence, the ocean of existence. It's the seen and the unseen, the visible stemming from the invisible that you can sense and feel. When you have mystical experiences like angelic visions or visitations from departed ancestors, you are experiencing your interconnectedness with the whole. Everything is interconnected.

Wholeness is a mind-blowing concept! It's big! It means there is only One Mind. Your consciousness exists within it, within One Mind. Whether or not you believe it, your thoughts contribute to and influence the world around you. Mostly, however, your thoughts contribute to and influence your own experience, as you have probably noticed.

Another important aspect of wholeness is that your life is unbreakable and indivisible. You cannot disconnect your mind from your body or your spirit. You cannot be split apart. Parts of you cannot be segregated and treated separately from the whole of you. You are not made up of separate pieces and parts; you are an integrated whole.

Wholeness is the reality of your self that is independent of your circumstances. As such, it is not about your age, your physical condition, your feelings, your accomplishments, or your genetics. You can ignore, but never eradicate, your wholeness. You can feel as if you are falling apart, but your wholeness can never be broken.

You are whole while traveling through varying conditions, and the whole you arrives at a new present. In order to focus on the present "you," you have to remain connected to the un-retouched and unencumbered you that predates your birth into humanity. Wholeness is the eternal spiritual you that is one with all that is—the original you that requires nothing in order to be whole. Neither ideal human parenting nor stress-free conditions are necessary for you to thrive. To thrive, you need only wholeness, which is the state of *being*, innate and irrepressible. You are wholeness itself.

It's one thing to acknowledge your wholeness. It's another, however, to feel whole in the midst of everyday human circumstances. As human beings, it makes sense for us to define our well-being based upon our circumstances. When times are good, we feel good. When times are tough, we sense that something is missing, wrong, or broken and we long to feel good again. Remember, however, that, because we are also spiritual beings, we can shift our awareness to our more subtle, but certain, identity. Knowledge of our wholeness needs to be reinforced by daily habits of thought and action. And healing is the action we take to claim our wholeness.

HEALING

Healing is natural. Except in rare cases, everyone has experienced healing. When you suffer the slightest injury, even a paper cut to your finger, healing begins before you even start to feel the sting. Blood platelets gather at the site and form a clot to stop the bleeding. Your immune system directs specialized cells to search for and gobble up infection. A protective scab forms. These and many other autonomic processes occur without the need for conscious direction from you.

Healing is also natural when we have experienced mental, emotional, or spiritual suffering. Every worrisome pattern of thought eventually resolves, just as every condition is a temporary occurrence that will pass. Innate strengths and capacities arise to meet these needs, time after time. To heal is to restore, to resolve, to realize; essentially, healing is simply a return to health. But the meaning of health, usually defined as freedom from illness or injury, is actually realizing *wholeness* and choosing well-being in every aspect of life. Health, seen in this light, includes your body, your mind, your emotions, and your spiritual concerns.

We may pray for healing, expect healing from our healthcare professionals, attend healing seminars, enroll in support groups, or try the latest home remedies. Healing is thus a consuming quest we embark on when we feel in need of it. To comprehend the meaning of healing, and how healing happens, is indeed a quest in itself—one no doubt prompted by an urgent need.

But remember: Our original nature is wholeness. We are not here to solve problems, learn lessons, endure as proof of our worth, right wrongs, fix broken parts of ourselves, or pursue anything that smacks of reform. We are here to seek healing as a forward, onward, and upward rise in our awareness and, therefore, our capacity for well-being. We are here to choose to live as well as possible every day.

If, as we propose, healing is not about curing conditions, how then can you define healing for yourself? Here are some definitions that have been useful to us.

Healing As Well-Being

Healing is, in fact, the fundamental idea behind well-being. It is a principle that informs behavior. As you hold to the idea of well-being and affirm the principle of health, it dawns in your mind. You begin to cooperate with the principle of health, choosing healthful thoughts and habits. You heal as you continue thinking and behaving in alignment with this principle.

Well-being is not predicated on having a flawless body. You *decide* whether well-being is possible for you, even as you must attend to physical symptoms and conditions. You *decide* whether health is less about a perfect body and more about overall well-being, or wholeness. The same is true of other conditions. To heal a prevailing sense of lack, study the principle of abundance. To heal resentment and bitterness, study the principle of harmony or love. To heal a sense of helplessness or futility, study the principles of self-mastery and order.

There is more to this process, however, than thinking a new thought or choosing a new behavior. Realization is a potent transformer, a spiritual activator. Holding steady to a principle requires dealing with various arguments against it that you may previously have believed to be true. "Who am I kidding? I'll never be well." "There is no cure for my disease." "God has abandoned me." Every time you notice contrary thoughts like these, return your mind to the principle of health, of well-being.

Wellness becomes a reality as you devote attention to it. Every moment of attention you give to it transforms you vibrationally as well as biochemically. But it takes practice. It takes repetition. In his book *Talks on Truth*, Charles Fillmore, cofounder of Unity, taught: "We want instantaneous healing of our diseases, but we are loath to sacrifice the mental habits that cause them." Many practices you will read about in this book are designed to assist you in activating your own sense of well-being.

One summer evening, Linda asked her husband to massage her back. As a therapist who gave as well as received massages, she was certain she had pulled a muscle and that a deep-tissue massage would relieve the spasm. Instead, when Giles applied pressure, she felt intense pain and realized something more serious was going on. They headed to the hospital, where Linda was diagnosed with pericarditis, a buildup of fluid around the heart probably caused by a virus. The remedy was weeks of bed rest.

Although the bed rest was welcome for the first few days, Linda soon became restless. It didn't help that she felt absolutely fine while sitting in bed propped up by pillows. But when she attempted to get up to prepare a meal or tried to do some laundry, she felt a crush of pain caused by the fluid around her heart. The doctor again stressed the need for bed rest and reinforced it with a threat of hospitalization. Once Linda understood that she could die from pericarditis, she cooperated with her body's need for respite and recovery. Moreover, an awareness of her mortality prompted in her an urgent need to understand her life in its fullness, beyond this present health challenge. She began to contemplate wholeness and well-being, principles she had been developing in her spiritual training.

Acknowledging the principles of wholeness and well-being, Linda shifted her focus from concern about her heart as an anatomical structure to an awareness of her heart as a representation of all that she loved about life. She committed herself to devoting more of her love energy toward her husband, her family, and her friends. Most important, she considered ways in which she could be more self-loving, including working less and playing more. By realizing the principles of wholeness and well-being, Linda reacquainted herself with the love that was an integral part of her, healing her life as her heart was healing.

Affirmation for Well-Being

My natural state of being is well-being.
No matter what I am sensing or feeling,
I am greater than this. I am whole.
My heart beats well-being.
My mind thinks well-being.
My body cooperates with well-being.
Well-being is my dominant intention,
My focus, and my experience.

Healing As Nurturing

Cultivating wholeness means nurturing and caring about all aspects of your being—physical, mental, emotional, and spiritual. While these aspects are not separate, they each contribute in different ways to your wholeness and require particular treatment. Just as you treat the different parts of your physical body—your hands, your hair, your digestive system—according to their needs, cultivating wholeness requires an unapologetic devotion to all the aspects of your being that make you *you*.

An inspiring example of nurturing wholeness comes from Unity's cofounder, Myrtle Fillmore, who was expected to die in her forties from tuberculosis. Instead, Myrtle engaged in specific healing practices, like meditation, prayer, affirmation, and mental discipline. In her meditation practice, she spoke directly to her internal organ systems—not merely her respiratory system, but each system in turn—encouraging them, appreciating them, and committing to take good care of them. This practice led her to examine her beliefs, attitudes, and actions, recalibrating them to nurture her wholeness.

Healing is too often focused on particular symptoms or on the primary site of an ailment. This narrow focus unfortunately leads to a shrunken view of life that is limited and impaired by a disease or other unwanted condition. When you nurture wholeness, however, you broaden your attention so that you view your circumstances within a framework of overall well-being. No matter the condition, whether related to health, prosperity, harmony in relationships, inner peace, or world peace, you heal by nurturing your original, true being—your wholeness.

Affirmation for Nurturing

I heal as I realize my innate capacity
To live with wholeness in mind.
I attend to, strengthen, and support
All aspects of my whole life.
With compassionate thoughts
And supportive actions,
I nurture my whole self.

Healing As Freedom

Freedom is at the heart of longing. Think about it. Longing for a cure is less about reacquiring a perfect body than it is about being free from symptoms and their limitations. Longing for reconnection with your first family is less about winning their regard than it is about freely holding your heart open again.

But, as the familiar saying goes: There is freedom from . . . and there is freedom to.

When you are reeling from confusion caused by the undue influence of external authorities like well-meaning friends and professional caregivers, imagine freeing yourself from the demands of their influence. Imagine enjoying the freedom to take their recommendations as information rather than direction. Imagine vetting them in the court of your inner discernment. For example, by freeing yourself from a story of inherited disease, you disconnect the cord tying your circumstances to past generations. You no longer carry your ancestors on your shoulders, adding weight to an already daunting condition. You are free instead to respond to the needs of today, unencumbered.

Collective consciousness is a term introduced by psychologist Carl Jung that describes the shared beliefs and judgments held by our dominant culture. Healing yourself may entail freeing yourself from all that the collective consciousness says about your own circumstances. Questioning common knowledge can be a helpful way to confront beliefs engrained in the collective consciousness and free yourself from them. For instance, consider our beliefs about aging. Whether we are conscious of it or not, we are constantly peppered with collective-consciousness beliefs that practically guarantee our bodies will betray us as we age, and that we will become increasingly dependent upon others as our faculties diminish. Imagine the healing possible when we disassociate ourselves from these beliefs!

When you are free from the tether of dominating collective thought, you are free to claim your wholeness. You heal when you are free from struggling against your conditions. Well-meaning friends often use fighting words and martial metaphors to encourage patients undergoing treatment for cancer. But, if you were so afflicted, would you really intend to war against your own body? Would you really gain by doing battle or feeling compelled to position yourself as a warrior? Imagine freeing yourself from this combative stance and opening yourself to the flow of a more expansive view of your life and your freedom. Imagine responding in harmony with your intention to live into wholeness.

To heal is to make peace with your past. When you free yourself from meaning-making about your past that interferes with your present, you become free to integrate supportive values from times gone by without being beholden to previous assumptions or paralyzed by horrors previously endured.

Affirmation for Freedom

Breathing easily, I free myself from false
  imaginings
Of lack or limitation.
Connecting to my innate wholeness,
I am free to experience the fullness of life today.
Understanding that I cannot be chained to
Or bound by my circumstances,
I soar freely, healed as I fully focus
On my passions and possibilities.

Healing As Evolution

To understand healing is to understand that life is never static and is always evolving. When we fall prey to erroneous notions of healing as an end point, we keep real healing at bay. To heal is not to achieve a final state of being after which you will live happily ever after. Healing, like wholeness, is ever-evolving.

One way you can conceptualize the evolutionary power of healing is to reflect on the messages inherent in your culture's origin stories. The creation story in Genesis bears similarities to creation myths found in oral and written accounts around the world. English translations of this text leave readers with the impression that creation was a once-upon-a-time event presided over by a creator deity. But these ancient writings were never meant to suggest that creation was an historic event that occurred at a single point in time. Aramaic bible scholar Neil Douglas-Klotz suggests, instead, that we look at life as an unfolding, ever-renewing beginning, rather than as a fixed, ideal end result. In Douglas Klotz' book *The Genesis Meditations*, Rabbi and kabbalah scholar Abraham Kook likewise encourages us to "sense creation not as something completed, but as constantly becoming, evolving, ascending."

Beginnings are built into our calendars. Historical and cultural anniversaries, holidays, and birthdays carry us on a current of newness and fresh starts. Yet, isn't every day truly a new beginning? Indeed, every moment? Every moment you choose healing, you begin again. And each new beginning builds momentum. Each new beginning causes you to evolve.

A spiral is often used to represent the momentum of evolution—not spiraling downward, but rather spiraling outward, opening or blossoming. Spirals are found among the earliest symbols drawn by human communities around the globe. They were used to represent the cyclical forces of nature and appear naturally in sunflowers, hurricanes, tornadoes, ocean waves, and nautilus shells. Spirals are evident as well in our fingerprints, our ear canals, and our DNA.

Spirals are associated with the feminine, creative, evolutionary force of infinite wisdom that lives within everyone. In human development from infancy toward maturity, our ability to think and make meaning naturally expands. Life goes from simple to complex. The view you have on any subject today is dependent upon all that you have learned and intuited along the way. It is a distinct view, a pinnacle view, based on your access to all that you have ever known.

We all know and love people who demonstrate the healing power of evolution. Perhaps some of your friends are in twelve-step programs, living "one day at a time." Today, you yourself may face familiar life themes—issues you have dealt with before, but now address with greater maturity and spiritual capacity to navigate your human challenges. This is how we spiral through life, healing and reclaiming our wholeness.

This Life Is Yours

Affirmation for Evolution

I begin this day in a spirit of beginningness,
Breathing fresh breath and thinking new thoughts.
My life is continually unfolding.
Today, if an issue arises that
I thought I had already healed,
I recognize that I meet the issue
From a fresh perspective,
That I am wiser and more mature
Than when I last encountered this challenge.
I begin again. I level-up. I evolve.

CHAPTER 2

The Value of Questioning

Blessed be the longing that brought you here and quickens your soul with wonder. . . .

—John O'Donohue, *To Bless the Space between Us*

We have established that healing is thinking and acting in ways that champion the truth of wholeness. For many, this new information runs contrary to the common assumption that an unwanted condition means that something is missing, wrong, or broken in their lives. In this chapter, we propose two significant questions to ask once you are ready for healing: *Why?* and *What do I want?* Your answers will lead you toward a deep understanding of healing and inspire you to know your innate wholeness. It may be tempting to accept your first responses and then move on. But we encourage you to ask yourself these questions again and again as you continue reading. Answering them in depth will inspire and motivate you to live as well as possible every day and lead you to your deepest knowing.

But first, let's examine how the dominant culture has led to viewing life, and circumstances, as flawed.

THE MINDSET OF INSUFFICIENCY

When we think, say, or hear the word "healing," we tend to associate it with the idea that something has gone wrong that needs to be righted; something is missing that needs to be found; something is broken that needs to be fixed. From our earliest experiences, we have been immersed in the idea that we are less than whole. But this idea itself is flawed. It sets us up to agree with the mindset that dominates our culture—the mindset of our own insufficiency. Entire systems have been built upon this mindset.

Countless religions have sprung from the premise that all manner of terrible conditions are beyond our control and that, in a state of powerlessness, we may find comfort believing in a God who has the power to relieve us of our burdens. Disease, disaster, decline, or death—anything gone wrong, really—arrives inexplicably at our doors. Or perhaps some deity brought them about for his or her own purposes. God could, if God would, heal us and our conditions as a favor, or as a reward, or as a compensation. In fact, you may believe that only God can save you from a fractured human existence.

Social systems are also complicit in this idea of brokenness. Consider the welfare programs intended to aid poor children and others unable to fend for themselves. The system was well-intentioned, born of kindness and caring. But over time, the system proved successful only at keeping the poor in their place. Linda experienced the negative impact of this system when working for an insurance company hiring mailroom and filing clerks for minimum wage. She hired a young woman fresh off welfare—a single mom with a couple of little ones at home. The new employee was filled with hope and delight at entering the workforce. Her joy soured within weeks, however, as she realized that her wages were woefully inadequate to meet her expenses, and that many of those expenses were no longer subsidized by the system. The costs of childcare, healthcare, professional clothing, and transportation now all had to be borne by her on a subsistence wage. The system was designed to be all or nothing. You got a job? You're off our rolls. The bright young woman eventually quit because she was smart enough to see that she could manage better on welfare than she could on her own.

Healthcare in Western culture is another system based in brokenness. When you go to the doctor because something seems wrong, the doctor is duty-bound to find something wrong. Linda found this out when she agreed to a physical a few years ago—a physical that became far more complicated than any she had previously undergone. So many vials of blood! Mammogram, bone density scan, colonoscopy, oh my! When she entered the doctor's office, she was feeling great—at her optimum weight and fitness, energetic and inspired. But her tests came back with negative indications and she was referred to an endocrinologist who, within minutes, convinced her that she was falling apart. "Your bones are deteriorating. You have nodules in your thyroid. Your blood sugar is too high. We need more tests, lots of tests."

Linda left the endocrinologist's office crushed and disillusioned. She had worked hard to build up her immune system, strengthen her musculoskeletal system, and normalize her weight. And for what? Eventually, more blood work revealed that many of the test results were either anomalies or false positives. Linda came away from the experience convinced that she had temporarily gotten caught in the web of a system *determined* to find something wrong with her.

Of course, we are all thankful for doctors and specialists when conditions call for their expertise. Most of us are not against medical care. But we are better served when we seek support for wellness while we are well and seek medical care judiciously and intentionally, always choosing the most natural methods that may be effective. Doctors who are knowledgeable about alternative treatments and who can give us plenty of options are the ones best able to guide us to healing. Western medicine at its best is life-supportive; at its worst, it perpetuates a mistaken belief in brokenness.

Mental healthcare is another system that tends to pathologize common human emotions and behaviors. The latest diagnostic manual for psychiatrists defines the grief that is appropriate after the death of a loved one as a mental illness. If you describe yourself as eccentric, distractible, or indecisive, an eager-to-please diagnostician is likely to name these idiosyncrasies as mental illnesses and prescribe powerful drugs to correct them. Alicia experienced this first-hand in college when a professor in an abnormal psychology class made the point that mothers who experience trauma, high stress, or emotional distress while pregnant may inflict cognitive, social, and behavioral challenges on their children. Now, we all long for answers and reasons that can justify how we feel and behave, especially when we believe that something is wrong. So, like any well-adjusted, emotionally stable young adult, Alicia immediately blamed her mother for everything wrong in her life, looking for an explanation of why she was the person she had become. Linda, being fully aware of the blame-the-parent trap, told Alicia how much she had loved being pregnant and that Alicia had come into this world knowing exactly who she was.

With every passing year, rapid advancements in information technology contribute to this culture of brokenness. Social media, broadcast news, and television shows all seem to highlight and exploit things that need fixing. Not only do these media outlets foster a culture of brokenness, they tend to shape the way we communicate with each other into exchanges that are polarizing and confrontational. We scrutinize and criticize those who do not see the world as we do. When new information surfaces that challenges our stated beliefs, we then struggle to clarify our own convictions. But when we post every troubling thought on social media, or co-opt other people's posts with our own agenda, or defend our position to the point of un-friending someone, we perpetuate the idea that something is missing, wrong, or broken.

Alicia once reacted to a post that a friend had shared about a celebrity with what she thought was a benign and funny comment. Then she heard a "ping" indicating that someone else had commented—someone she did not know who was a friend of her friend. When she saw that this person had refuted her comment, she experienced a rush of emotions. She was ready to hulk out! She didn't like the feeling of being questioned when she believed she was right. But she paused long enough to remind herself why she generally preferred not to engage in these online exchanges and realized there was no need to continue the debate or make an enemy out of a stranger.

So she responded gingerly and respectfully, and still got her point across. We all have the ability to choose how to respond in this kind of situation. Does defending a position add something to the discussion or take away from it? Does it lead to healing and evolution, or does it perpetuate the assumption that something is missing, wrong, or broken in the world?

The subtle, but powerful, influence of the collective consciousness affects everyone, even though, at times, we may be unaware of it. These subliminal forces work to convince us that disease is an enemy to be battled, that having enough is a perpetual challenge, and that suffering is inevitable. When we participate in this culture of brokenness, we lean away from our innate wholeness. When this happens, healing has to become our priority.

WHY?

Every human being is subject to times of joy and times of sorrow; times of celebration and times of grief; times of plenty and times of scarcity; times of success and times of failure. Emotional highs and lows are guaranteed within the fullness of human experience. Everyone suffers. And we all want to know why. When your good life goes off the rails, or when you seem to be accosted by a parade of calamities, or when the unexpected and unwanted life-threat occurs, you want to know why. And the way you answer that question determines whether you see yourself as victim or victor—whether you ultimately are weakened or strengthened by the experience.

Humans have been asking and trying to answer this question since the beginning of time. Answers to it have been shaped by thought leaders and storytellers in every era. And seeking a determinate cause for an unwanted condition often assumes that, once you pinpoint the cause, you will be able to heal the condition. Causation, however, is a subjective concept. Depending on the worldview of the questioner, a cause can be determined to be natural, mental, moral, or supernatural. In fact, selecting a particular cause from the spectrum of possibilities says more about the questioner than it does about the condition being examined.

Spiritual teachers, understandably, often avoid asking the question entirely. They tell us to ask a different question. You'll never get a satisfactory answer, they say, or you'll only blame God, or the alignment of the planets, or, worse, yourself. But the question persists. And the answer that makes the most sense to you may leave others scratching their heads in skepticism.

Below we present four common answers to this question, followed by the one we prefer. As you read, pay attention to your own gut reactions, arguments, and agreements. Challenge answers that conform to your current understanding and try to move beyond them.

Invisible Forces

Prehistoric explanations for illness and other unwanted conditions conformed to a worldview of life as mostly mysterious. Invisible, unknowable forces controlled everything from weather to reproduction. When something unwanted occurred, it was logical to believe that it was caused by a supernatural power, a spirit, or a deity. Ancient Middle Eastern as well as European cultures believed illness was the work of evil spirits. Sickness and evil were bound together, interchangeable in some languages and contexts. Medieval Christianity even assigned a particular illness to each of the seven deadly sins, regarding illness as divine punishment.

Lest we laugh off these invisible causes for disease and misfortune and relegate them to prehistoric superstition, consider present-day explanations offered by religion. Biblical literalists insist that sickness and distress are endemic to a broken and fallen humanity, suggesting that God not only allows, but actually sends, sickness and distress as punishment for humanity's inherently sinful nature. Another explanation tries to convince us that sickness and distress are lessons sent by a didactic God for our own good or our instruction.

The problem with believing that sickness and distress are conditions caused by evil spirits or in response to personal sin is that we then must rely upon the very spirit or deity who has caused our condition to heal it! We have to appease this spirit with self-sacrifice and penance. God first hurts us; then, if we are lucky, God heals us.

> Come, let us return to the Lord. He has
> torn us to pieces, but he will heal us; he has
> injured us but he will bind up our wounds.
> (Hosea 6:1 NIV)

A kinder, gentler answer is proposed by religious claims that sickness and distress come to us for the glory of God. In this belief system, God does not give us conditions to hurt us; instead, our sickness and distress give God a reason to heal us and display his power and glory. If you tend toward fatalism, you may believe that only God knows why, and God must have a good reason.

Inexplicably, in most expressions of Christianity, suffering is not only caused by sin; it is also the remedy for sin. To suffer is, therefore, noble. Relief from suffering comes by way of salvation or acknowledging Jesus Christ as Lord and Savior, which absolves the believer of sin and paves the way for an eternity in heaven. Similarly, Islam and Judaism suggest that suffering is caused by the will of God, and faith is strengthened by enduring hardship. Can you recognize the effects of theology and religious culture on your own answers to this question?

Natural Imbalances

Ancient Greek physicians like Hippocrates held that disease was caused by an imbalance of the four humors: blood, phlegm, black bile, and yellow bile. The humors were associated with the four elements: air, water, earth, and fire. Traditional Chinese Medicine seeks to restore physical balance and harmony with therapies that adjust the body's vital energy, or *qi*. In Western medicine, genetics, environment, biochemistry, and/or physiology are presumed causes of physical or mental illness.

Personal Sin

But if God does not cause sickness and distress, then we must cause it ourselves! Many modern theories about the cause of physical and mental afflictions borrow from religiously induced guilt. You may not name it "sin," but your own stinking thinking, you believe, is the cause of your ills. Metaphysics as taught in various New Thought disciplines identifies the human mind as the origin point for human troubles. New Thought teaching taken out of context can thus appear to point a finger of blame back at the thinker. But remember: "I am my own worst enemy" does not necessarily mean that you have caused your condition.

Complexity

Holistic medicine, as ancient as Ayurveda and as modern as Naturopathy, regards biological imbalance as a plausible cause for disease and distress. But these disciplines, along with Traditional Chinese Medicine, chiropractic, and various energy-healing modalities, continue searching for causal complexity. Holistic medicine treats the whole person rather than seeking a single cause. "Body, mind, and spirit" is the refrain for holistic methodologies. Imbalances? Probably. Self-defeating attitude? Likely. Spiritual void? Perhaps. All are connected and contribute to the experience of someone who is in the midst of an unwanted condition. But remember: To experience a condition is not the same as to cause it.

The Law of Attraction

We prefer a different answer, grounded in what we call the "law of attraction." The law of attraction is the spiritual counterpart of gravity—a law of nature that is true for everyone, every time. All matter is subject to gravity. All things get pulled toward a gravitational center. Spiritually, love is the gravitational center of life. All thought, feeling, and action get pulled toward love by the power of magnetism, harmony, and unity. This means that all our feelings about whatever happens draw us toward love. In other words, love is the anchor point of life. It is tied to our desires, whether those desires are born from wanted or unwanted experiences.

A white woman, whose wife and daughter were African American, contacted Linda after reading her books. She and her family repeatedly came face-to-face with our culture's social deficits with regard to homophobia and racism. She liked what Linda had written about the law of attraction—known as the "law of mind action" in the Unity tradition. In her book *Divine Audacity*, Linda decribes how that law works:

> The good news about the law of attraction is that love, the great magnet, is what pulls us in every circumstance, good and bad. Situations are not being sent our way by some other source. We, as love, go into all circumstances. We attract ourselves into the details of our life, for love. The light of love wants to shine, to heal, to transform, to unify, and to harmonize.

The woman could not, however, see how the law could be applied to social problems like homophobia and racism. How could love allow hate? Her visceral resistance to this idea is not an uncommon reaction.

The law of attraction states that we are the creators of our own experience and of our reality. But this is too often misinterpreted to mean that we create our *circumstances*. If this were true, it would mean that we instigate or invite unwanted circumstances. It would mean that we create disease, heartbreaks, and devastating events. We do not! Confusion about the law of attraction leads to unnecessary self-condemnation and despair.

Misinterpretation of the law of attraction extends to a further belief that we gravitate toward unwanted conditions in order to learn lessons, or that we attract conditions so we will give them our attention and grow through them. We do not! This all-too-familiar explanation arises from prevailing religious messaging about a God who hurts us in order to teach us—because he or she loves us.

Some say we attract bad things when we are influenced by a collective consciousness of fear. It is plausible, for example, that widespread fear of other cultures may encourage us to spew hateful messages to those we perceive as different. Although we judge these hateful messages as wrong, those influenced by a collective consciousness of fear may consider them reasonable. No one likes an explanation that seems to excuse bad behavior. Yet, in fact, each of us determines what is bad and what is not, according to our values and beliefs.

The woman experiencing homophic and racist behavior may, in fact, have been inclined to excavate her own unacknowledged biases. It may even have been useful for her to do so. While dining in public with her multiethnic family, she may have felt nervous about how they would be perceived, or defensive as she looked into the eyes of other diners. If she had been able to recognize that, her unease could have been instructive. Instead, however, she leaped from her awareness of unease to a conclusion that her nervousness or defensiveness caused the unpleasant encounter. We know we are vibrational beings and that our vibrations permeate the environment. We are told, therefore, that other people's nervousness or defensiveness attracts ours. But does it? Or is there another, more useful, explanation?

Bad things that happen in the world, and the troubling conditions we experience, are contrasts. They stand out because they appear opposite to what we value or hold as beliefs. But opposites attract. Mass acts of terrorism assault our ideal of communal security; being denied equal rights runs counter to our sense of belonging. Illness contrasts with our belief in innate wholeness and health. Love, the magnetizing power, exerts a continuous pull on contrasting values so that they can be resolved and harmonized.

In other words, your inner being, your core identity, is love and nothing *other*. You long to live in harmony with all of life. You live to be secure and free within, as well as with, all that is around you. You desire the inner peace derived from feeling at home in the world, perceiving nothing and no one as being against you. Anything you perceive to be not love becomes visible, striking out like a flash of lightning in a dark sky. It's not as if you ask for it or cause it; it's just the nature of contrasts. They grab your attention.

In the case of the woman who repeatedly encountered bigoted behavior, it seems clear that bigotry stood in strong contrast to her values of open-mindedness and inclusiveness. No one could blame her for fleeing the scene or throwing back some choice words of her own. Anchored as she is to her true nature—love—she searches for a satisfactory explanation about why she and her family came to this experience, and how she could be the key to its resolution.

Remember: You do not cause bad things to come your way. A looming mysterious force—call it God or fate—does not send awful circumstances your way as if you deserved them because of your private worries and judgments. Your innermost unknown-to-you thoughts and feelings do not cause bad things to happen to you. The self-blame game—what we call "metaphysical malpractice"—is destructive rather than constructive. It leads to self-condemnation, a position from which you cannot move forward. You get locked into it, paralyzed by a belief that you have brought about and deserve your suffering.

But if you are not responsible for creating bad things that happen, what *is* your responsibility? The law of attraction claims that you are responsible for your *experience*. And how you respond to that experience matters to you. Your response is either in keeping with your values and beliefs, or it is not. When your response is harmonious with your values and beliefs, you feel better.

When you behave against your own values and beliefs, you feel worse.

The woman who suffered from her experience of bigotry is not responsible for having created bigotry or for having brought it upon herself and her family. Her only responsibility—her *response*-ability—lies in how she reacts. A response likely not in concert with her values and beliefs might be: "I will have to be on alert from now on so that I can protect my daughter and my wife. It's an unfriendly world for us. We are not safe. Next time, I will spew hateful messages right back." A response more aligned with her values and beliefs might be: "I look forward to living in a caring and kind community where all people are included. I will do my best to include others, even those who think and act so differently from me, even someone spewing hateful messages. I will not give back bigotry for bigotry."

We admit that it may not be easy to answer hatred with love. It may not be easy, but it is possible. Why? Because our very nature is love. Likewise, it may not be easy to respond to sickness by focusing on all that is going well, but it is possible. Why? Because wholeness is our true nature.

WHAT DO I WANT?

When you feel ill, it's understandable that you want to feel better. When you feel defeated, you want to feel successful. So it seems as if it should be easy to answer the question: "What do I want?" You want a desired outcome; you want to eliminate present conditions; you want a miraculous remission. You think about healing as returning to a time when you felt whole. But we maintain that there are deeper, truer, more compelling answers that you can turn to in the midst of unwanted conditions. We believe that asking yourself what you want can lead toward deep longings and true desires that will help you commit to the kinds of practices that will foster health and well-being.

What are you longing for? What are you agonizing over? Health? Peace of mind? Rewarding work? Satisfying relationships? These are all universal desires felt by all members of our human family. The more you believe you are missing out on one or more of these conditions, the more you may long for them. You may long to lose weight, to complete your college degree, or to accomplish any number of goals. More subtly, you may long to be free of compulsive behaviors, to master time, or to become more assertive.

The fact is that longing is natural to us all. At the heart of all humanity is a perpetual stirring of desire. In the wake of any moment's satisfaction, longing builds again, only to crest as the next possibility takes shape. And every longing is necessary, because every longing is tied to our irrepressible wholeness. Every deep desire reflects a longing to know our divine identity—a realization that we can not be separate from God or from others or from life. A conviction that we are whole within the whole. That we *be*-long. *Be*-longing is fulfilling our longing, realizing what we are and that we are therefore at home.

In *A Blue Fire*, the late archetypal psychologist James Hillman wrote this of the connection between love and longing:

> Why do we focus so intensely on our problems? What draws us to them? Why are they so attractive? They have the magnet power of love: somehow we desire our problems; we are in love with them much as we want to get rid of them. . . . Problems sustain us—maybe that's why they don't go away. What would a life be without them? Completely tranquilized and loveless, too. There is a secret love hiding in each problem.

A Dream of Self-Mastery

At age fifty-nine, Linda experienced an excruciating longing that gnawed at her. She recognized it in a familiar refrain of self-disgust related to her seeming inability to regulate her weight, control her appetite, and exercise her body. She wanted to repress it, but each time she tried, years of practiced self-condemnation wriggled to the surface of her awareness. Finally, her dream of self-mastery prompted her to take action. She decided to *be in* her feelings of self-condemnation rather than to numb them or distract herself from them.

A picture of herself at age sixteen haunted her—an image of twin pony tails framing a smiling face as a slim young girl walked in a field at summer camp. How had she never noticed that, despite thinking of herself as "hippo hips" and "thunder thighs"—names given to her by her brothers—she had been a beautiful, petite teenager? She found herself longing to know that teenager—wanting to *be* her. She yearned to experience her hopes, her innocence, her passion, her wholeheartedness. She wanted to feel the way she should have felt as a sixteen-year-old! She was stunned to realize the terrible damage done by her own dysmorphic body image. She had become as large as she had always imagined herself to be. She had lost and gained weight dozens of times, but willpower always failed her. She felt defeated.

"When I committed to *being* in my longing," Linda recalls, "I started to remember early life experiences and the decisions I had made based on them. When, as a five-year-old, my mother and aunt laughed during my dance class, I convinced myself they were laughing at me and that I was irretrievably awkward. I nurtured a dread that I would take after an aunt who, at age sixty, resembled a squat quarterback. As I went through puberty, I began to accept the limits of my genetics, which I believed cursed me with a double dose of curvy hips and thick thighs." These and other memories began to inform Linda's perception of her physical appearance. When she looked in the mirror, she saw a distorted image much like that seen in a fun house. Repeated attempts at dieting and an aversion to exercise convinced her that she would never achieve the body she wanted. So she just gave up.

Then Linda came to a startling realization. "At the time," she explains, "I was deep into inquiry about my spiritual power of will, consumed with learning about my power to choose, commit, and be willing. Imagine my discomfort when it dawned on me that I had been saying to myself, not 'I will,' but 'I will not.' Once I recognized that, I became willing to be willing, and this unleashed many other inner capacities." Soon, Linda started questioning every limited and false idea she had harbored about her body. This breakthrough tipped the scales, spiritually. She committed herself to heal spiritually first and then let her restored consciousness guide her. She knew she was on the right track when, instead of feeling discouraged and defeated, she started to feel interested and curious. She paid attention to the eating habits of people she admired—people who ate with gusto, who loved good food. She observed women who wore their clothing well and exuded beauty. She made a point of noticing muscular definition, shapeliness, strength, flexibility, and vitality.

Then two things happened that prompted Linda to take action. The first she describes as wonderful: "I felt my energy shift. Seeds of 'I will' had grown into tender, tentative sprouts of willingness, making me feel enthusiastic, hopeful, and free of the conflict in my head." The second she remembers as terrible: "A dear friend and colleague died. When I learned of this, my heart sank into sorrow. But in the midst of that sorrow, I suddenly heard the voice of my friend encouraging me: 'Your new life starts now.' And I declared myself willing to be willing."

A Lesson about Longing

A spiritual teacher was meditating near the edge of a lake when a young man approached him and asked to become his student. When the teacher asked why, the young man replied: "I long to find God." The teacher leapt up from his seat, pulled the young man into the water by his collar, and held his head under until he felt the young man flailing for survival. Then he lifted him out of the water and, ignoring his anger, asked pointedly: "What did you most want when your head was under water?" Livid, the young man screamed: "Air! I wanted air!" "Very well," replied the teacher. "Go home and come back to see me when you long for God as much as you just longed for air" (*spiritual-short-stories.com*).

Longing is an uncomfortable state of being that we want to leave behind as quickly as possible. But the power of longing is in its persistence—a gnawing feeling that strikes us again and again. And when that feeling of longing nags at us, it's easy to wave the white flag and say: "Alright! I will do anything to send you on your way."

Irish poet John O'Donohue encouraged us to accept our longing as "divine urgency." The more seriously you take your deep and pressing longings, the more you will be positioned to take constructive action. And that action begins with *being*. As 20th-century metaphysician Neville Goddard taught:

> The end of yearning is to *be*. Your concept of yourself can only be driven out of consciousness by another concept of yourself. By creating an ideal in your mind, you can identify yourself with it until you become one and the same with the idea, thereby transforming yourself into it.

Once your longing is stimulated—knocking on your door, so to speak—you can begin to determine your preferred identity. Will you consider yourself an ill person or a well person? Will you define yourself by your circumstances or by your strengths? In the next chapter, we'll examine the amazing power of your mind that enables you to choose wholeness as your true identity.

CHAPTER 3

The Power
of Mind

If your mind is expansive and unfettered, you will
find yourself in a more accommodating world, a
place that's endlessly interesting and alive. That
quality isn't inherent in the place but in your state
of mind.

—Pema Chödrön, *Living Beautifully
with Uncertainty and Change*

The bad news, and the good news, is that you are powerful. Actually, it is all good news! You are powerful by
virtue of your mind. You may be thinking you are out
of your mind, or your mind is out of your control. You
may be experiencing life from a well-practiced mindset
of helplessness. But no matter what you have thought

about your mind, it is the seat of your power. And you are in control. In this chapter, we'll examine the magnificent power of your mind to know your wholeness, to shape your thoughts, and to transform your experience. Once you know more about the power of your mind, you can use that power to awaken some of your amazing inner resources—the spiritual capacities that allow you to heal.

THE INFLUENCE OF THOUGHTS

Thoughts held in the mind are real—invisible, yet felt as vibration. In other words, the fact that you cannot see your thoughts does not mean they are unreal or insignificant. Thoughts have real effects, just like the atmosphere around you, which is primarily invisible, yet felt. Although you may not have access to someone else's thoughts, you can feel either comfortable or uncomfortable in their presence.

Predominant, repetitive thoughts tend to become beliefs. Your dominant worldview, outlook, and attitudes solidify into beliefs that give shape to the world you see and experience. You may be harboring unconscious beliefs that began as messages you internalized in childhood. Once, in a class on the principles of prosperity, Linda reflected on messages from childhood that became operative in her adult experience. "Money doesn't grow on trees." "We can't afford that." "There's only so much to go around." "Money is the root of all evil." When she realized that these early messages had become beliefs about money and prosperity for her, she understood why she was worried about money much of the time. She had learned, and practiced, a way of thinking that led to poverty consciousness. When we begin to question what we believe about health, well-being, abundance, God, or anything else, we may recall messages that led us to have limiting, diminishing, or pessimistic ideas about many aspects of life.

Thoughts that are strongly held and long practiced become beliefs that have definite effects on us and on those around us. They broadcast energy and are imbued with unique vibrational frequencies that impact us and the world we live in, contributing to either fear or faith. Although a single, fleeting thought may have only a small effect, a persistent stream of thoughts can have an enormous impact. Consider how a Facebook post gone viral about a single case of a communicable disease can set off mass panic. Spreading thoughts and prayers, as frustrating as those sentiments may seem when you feel the need for social action, are known to have positive effects.

Thoughts are impactful simply because we are all interconnected. An intricate, delicate interactivity takes place continuously in non-visible, non-tangible reality— at the level of energy or vibration, at the level of thought.

We are all integral parts of this whole. As such, we influence and are influenced by everything and everyone. There is no such thing as separation between you and everything, between you and everyone. You are, and we all are, of One Mind.

THE INFLUENCE OF FEELINGS

Like thoughts, feelings are impactful. They can be suppressed, but not erased. Feelings are invisible, yet you can sense when someone feels sad or angry or loving. They are fleeting; they come and they go, seemingly with a will of their own. Feelings, however, are messengers. They can help you learn about yourself, recognize what is important to you, and, especially, understand who and what you are.

As we mature, we recognize that emotions and feelings come and go; they are temporary. There is a reason why we describe them using metaphors of the weather. We weather emotional storms; we let go a flood of tears; we are sometimes cold as ice. When we feel relief, we say that the fog has lifted, the clouds have parted, or the storm has passed. Buddhist teacher Thich Nhat Hanh taught that feelings come and go "like clouds in a windy sky." Nineteenth-century poet-mystic Kahlil Gibran wrote: "The feelings we live through in love and in loneliness are simply, for us, what high tide and low tide are to the sea." But, although they are fleeting, unwanted emotions can behave like barn swallows that return season after season to the underbelly of your back porch. These recurring unwanted feelings are personified in the film *What about Bob?* in a character who makes a pest of himself and will not stay away.

Allowing these feelings to become a constructive part of your quest for wholeness becomes a delicate process when you recognize that they are fleeting. You can practice this by thinking of your emotions as waves breaking and receding, as Gibran describes. You just have to learn to recognize when your feelings have crested, like a woman knowing she is at the height of a birthing contraction. Of course, if you suffer from acute or relentless pain, we are not suggesting that you can easily blow past it. Pain is a physical as well as an emotional phenomenon— an emotion that is processed in the brain and sensed in the body. Whether in relationship to an observable injury or an unobservable trigger, pain is real.

You may find, however, that, when you have break-through pain that is hard to manage with prescribed medication, it may help to notice the feelings of relief you experience in the moments between pain sensations. In the chapters to come, we suggest specific practices that can support you through pain so that you can experience the fleeting nature of these feelings and focus on the relief that comes as they pass.

Unreliable Chameleons

Feelings can appear masked as truths, but they are not truths. They are chameleons—unreliable and unreasonable. The only meaning feelings have is the meaning you make of them by connecting them to your beliefs. Unlike thoughts, feelings are irrational and uncontrollable. They are unpredictable and sometimes unrelated to the moment; they often arrive unbidden.

Tears can convey sorrow, joy, pain, confusion, or a sense of being overwhelmed. The cute baby video that touches you today may not move you on another day. You can be rolling along just fine and then . . . *thwack!* You are on your knees, crushed by a pressing grief. A stunning scene in a motion picture may plunge the rest of the audience into surprised silence, while you are the only one laughing hysterically. If you wonder about your sanity when you find yourself in the throes of an uncontrollable emotion, take heart in knowing that you cannot predict your feelings or reason with them. It is entirely okay, maybe even celebratory, to let your feelings flow.

Indicators, Not Directors

Feelings are indicators, not directors. They have no inherent power. The more familiar and frequent your feelings, the more inclined they are to push you toward particular actions. In fact, your feelings actually can assist you by pointing you toward meaning and purpose. Every time you make meaning of a particular feeling, you learn about what is important to you and what you most desire. Freedom is feeling what you feel without judging it as bad, misguided, or inappropriate.

Anger is a good example of an emotion that is an indicator rather than a director. When you feel a wave of anger after another driver cuts in front of you nearly causing an accident, your anger need not be a message telling you to behave rudely in return. As compelling as these feelings may be, acting on the basis of them alone can be reactionary—and reflexive action, or reaction, can be dangerous. It can also be self-defeating. It would be unwise, for example, if your physician tells you your present symptoms are unrelated to cigarette smoking, to react by resuming a habit you worked hard to eliminate.

When you understand that feelings are indicators, you allow yourself to feel what you feel fully. You come to understand that they can help you make meaning of a situation or an emotion before taking any next step. When you *choose* your next step rather than simply reacting, you are being responsive and *response*-able. Your actions flow from insight gained, understanding realized by the meaning you have made of your feelings. Actions follow feelings. Let your actions be informed and inspired.

Self-Discovery

The key to discovering the true you is to appreciate the distinction between "I feel" and "I am." Making this distinction can connect you to the true you—the you that exists beyond your feelings. As Kahlil Gibran wrote:

> Many of us spend our whole lives running from feeling with the mistaken belief that you cannot bear the pain. But you have already borne the pain. What you have not done is feel all you are beyond that pain.

Remember, the true you exists beyond your conditions. The true you is fully human and fully divine, wholeness itself. One of the most powerful feelings of disconnection you can experience is separation from self.

Describing her life as a biracial child of the Eighties, Alicia recalls her longing to fit in, to be defined. Near the end of second grade, her family moved to a small suburb of Omaha where you could count the number of other black children on two hands. At first, others were intrigued by her blackness and Alicia made friends quickly. But it wasn't long before she began to experience an undertone of "otherness" in little digs or questions that may have been intended as harmless, but to her felt like tiny burrs that cling and then prick just as much when you pull them off.

Alicia grew into adolescence with a heightened awareness that she was not safe everywhere she went. She loathed going out with her family because she felt they were always on display. It was particularly difficult to be seen with just her white mother, and she began a slow process of pulling away from family at a young age. She learned to cope with the ignorance and intolerance around her by trying to erase her blackness. When she was fifteen, however, and starting to date, she heard the message she had been sending herself all those years come back to her loud and clear. When one of her dates introduced her to his mother, who was obviously surprised by the color of her skin, he said: "Don't worry, Mom; she doesn't act black." Screech! Halt! What did that even mean?

Alicia realized in that moment that her dismissive attitude about her identity somehow gave others permission to pardon, rather than accept, her blackness—and that woke her up. She realized that she had to send a new message to herself that the color of her skin would never equate to her worthiness—but being black was to be celebrated. And she realized that her feelings of inadequacy were rooted in a void where the rich histories, wisdom, and stories of her father's family should have been. When she reconnected with that history in adulthood, she was able to embrace her true self and reconnect with her wholeness.

Thoughts and feelings are universal. Everyone thinks and everyone feels. As you process and respond to your own unique thoughts and emotions, you gain access to a greater, more expansive, infinite, and universal resource: the power of One Mind.

ONE MIND

We are of One Mind! One infinite, universal intelligence! You may think of it as God, or the ideal, or the noble, or the sacred. Within the One Mind lies the definition of and full potential for wholeness, abundance, harmony, equanimity, and fulfillment of all that can be considered ultimate truth. The good news you need to acknowledge during periods when you distrust your own thoughts is that your mind does not exist in isolation. It is connected to and is, essentially, one with the whole. Your mind is an individualization of One Mind, which is universal, shared intelligence.

To heal is to attune your thinking to One Mind, to elevate human thought to the ideal, the noble, or the sacred—to shift your focus from pessimistic, non-productive thoughts and beliefs to supportive, constructive ones. Father Edward Flanagan, founder of Boys Town, knew the healing power of the mind. He believed that every child could be a productive citizen if given love, a home, an education, and a trade. He welcomed boys discarded by their families and communities because he was convinced that "there are no bad boys." There are only bad environment, bad training, bad example, and bad thinking (*boystown.org*). He proved the power of the mind by reversing grim statistics for thousands of young men in his lifetime. His work continues today for the benefit of both boys and girls.

Mind and matter are not separate phenomena—a truth proven by science in recent decades. Contrary to theories from the Sixties, we now know that atoms and molecules arranged into physical form are not the basis of reality. The basis of reality is *consciousness*. Invisible thoughts, beliefs, expectations, and intentions create visible reality. Anyone who criticizes you for meditating, affirming, and imagining your way to healing has not yet experienced the power of mind.

Your mind is an amazing phenomenon and you are absolutely capable of harnessing its power. You can heal at the level of thought. When you heal your thoughts, you heal your experience. When you heal your experience, you positively change your relationship to your circumstances. Whether or not your circumstances improve or resolve at the pace you desire, you are no longer their victim. You experience wholeness, abundance, harmony, equanimity—in short, well-being.

The minutest particles of life in the cells of your body respond to practices that elevate mind and mood. Of course, they respond just as obediently to negative practices like self-condemnation or desperation. Nonetheless, that the life in your body responds to your persistent thought processes is cause for celebration, because it means that the power is within *you* to heal your life.

To heal worries about money and having enough—typically considered "poverty consciousness"—you can deliberately focus on conditions of plenty. Pause to notice plenty of water flowing out of the tap, or hundreds of wildflowers by the side of the road, or endless breaths entering and leaving your body. Bathe in feelings of appreciation for whatever you have right now. Give away something meaningful, whether a material object, a share of your money, or a portion of your time. Affirm your rightful place in the continual ebb and flow, the circulation, of life. In his book *Prosperity*, Charles Fillmore enjoins us to "cultivate the habit of thinking about abundance everywhere present," not only in our imaginations, but in the world around us as well. The same approach can lead to healing a disease-centric mentality, disharmony in a relationship, chronic anxiety, or other experiences stemming from your circumstances.

Human thinking has its limitations, however. As Carolyn Myss warns us in her book *Defy Gravity*:

> You cannot ask your mind to be other than what it is: a reason-seeking instrument. You must draw upon another part of yourself to transcend the

stubbornly reasoning mind that seeks vengeance for being humiliated or continually convinces you that you are entitled to more than what you have in this life. Such a mind is filled with toxins and it, too, needs healing. You must defy your mind, rise above it.

THE POWER TO PIVOT

The human brain is accomplished at spinning. Brain power is built upon repeated, related thoughts. You spin in worry over your aging parents' changing needs, your doctor's concern about a recent blood test, that confusing conversation you had yesterday with a coworker, or another news report of mass violence. But, in healing, it is as important to access the mystical, intuitive, spiritual nature of your being as it is to involve your conscious mind. It is important to become masterful at *pivoting* between intellectual and intuitive wisdom.

It is not easy to redirect your thoughts once they get to spinning. But you can do it by learning to pivot. Ruminating on a subject builds your capacity to envision and to act, perhaps even to improve circumstances. This has always been true, and it has proven beneficial throughout the ages. We can rightfully claim to have helped humans evolve because of our power to problem solve—a pattern set in ancient times when natural threats had to be met in order to survive. But problem-solving and intellectual thought have their limits. Thankfully, we now know that we are *more* than our brains. We are as spiritual as we are intellectual. And by focusing on our spiritual nature—by pivoting from the intellect to the intuition—we can bypass our spinning brains.

Charles Fillmore emphasized the pivotal nature of consciousness. The threefold nature of humanity, he taught, is spirit, soul, and body. The soul is the aspect of being that includes conscious thought and awareness. It derives inspiration either from the body (our circumstances and conditions) or the spirit (God-consciousness, One Mind, or universal intelligence). Pivoting toward the spirit is the "golden key"—a term first coined by Emmet Fox, a popular 20th-century spiritual leader—to realizing our wholeness. Spirit is our "God-Self," he taught, our divine identity. Spirit is the nature of God—think of it as *godness*—individualized, innate, and immutable. You can also think of it as your true self, your *real* self. Whereas the body and its conditions are temporary and finite, godness, or the real self, is eternal and infinite. By pivoting your awareness toward the eternal and infinite, you boost your brain power exponentially. Suddenly, your view becomes vast and that which seemed impossible becomes possible.

When you apply Fox's golden key—for instance, when you catch yourself thinking about your aging parents' changing needs—you pivot your attention away from thoughts that perpetuate worry so you can focus instead on godness or the real self. You breathe deeply, in prayerful awareness. In this state of spiritual realization, you connect with godness or the real self and can claim your divine identity. You open to the spaciousness of spiritual reality, which inspires your sense of direction. Divine ideas occur to you. You feel creative as well as relieved.

When you are attuned to godness or the real self, you discontinue the human perception of lack and limitation inherent in circumstances. Human deficits lose their power and you are no longer mesmerized by your circumstances. You recognize that the power that you previously perceived to be outside of you is in fact both your source and inner resource. Mental capacity and biochemistry align and you find you are capable of healing by transforming thought and matter (which follows thought). With practice, you get incrementally better at shifting power from a finite condition to an infinite capacity.

Alicia had an experience that led her to recognize this power at a workshop on developing self-leadership skills. When she chose "integrity" and "innovation" as two core values she wanted to pursue, she began to wonder about her choice of "integrity." Discussing it with the instructor, she realized she had chosen it because she valued congruency, which she defined as harmony between her thoughts and actions, and honesty in her relationships with others. The instructor suggested she substitute the word "authenticity," which she defined as speaking and

choose one in order to create it. You have to limit—pluck, define, shape, and name—one divine idea in order for it to come alive in your experience.

We unconsciously limit a warehouse full of groceries to our shopping list or our spending limit when we go to the store. We limit multiple choices of medications based upon our physician's prescription, on contraindications or known side effects, and on whether our insurance will cover it or there will be out-of-pocket costs. We limit our desires every time we imagine the perfect next automobile or sweetheart. In fact, we *must* limit them in order to imagine them, to give shape and particularity to them. If we didn't, we would not be able to recognize them or select them. And we do this by having faith in our inner resources, which allow us to create the conditions for healing and wholeness.

CHAPTER 4

Draw Upon Your Inner Resources

Though I do not believe that a plant will spring
up where no seed has been, I have great faith in a
seed. . . . Convince me that you have a seed there,
and I am prepared to expect wonders.

—Henry David Thoreau, *Faith in a Seed*

We have defined wholeness and established that the
conditions of your life set the scene for your desire to
heal. Now we turn to your inner resources or spiritual
capacities, the qualities you can draw upon to heal.
These capacities are not passive or lurking in the background; they are active forces that support your healing.
Charles Fillmore described them as inherent, yet dormant
unless we activate them. We identify these twelve inner

resources here as faith, imagination, understanding, will, zeal, power, love, wisdom, order, strength, release, and life. You can find a contemporary explanation of these spiritual capacities, also referred to as lights or powers, in Linda's book, *Divine Audacity: Dare to Be the Light of the World*.

In this chapter, we'll explore the role of each of these spiritual capacities in healing. Start by studying any one power. Work with it each day, reading the affirmations and practicing the power. You will be amazed at the ways your thoughts and experiences begin to shift.

FAITH:
PERCEPTION, CONVICTION, EXPECTANCY

Faith is much more than belief. In fact, faith is not a belief in any power that is external or *other*. Faith is your ability to see beneath the surface and beyond the appearance of any circumstance. Faith begins with your perception. It gives you mystical eyes that distinguish the real from the unreal. You believe because you have a view on desired possibilities and are faithfully focused on living expectantly. It's like pregnancy. Even when you know the gender of a yet-unborn child, there is still a lot you don't know about its birth. Yet you live in expectation, doing all you can to prepare for what comes next.

When Linda enrolled in a local workshop on perception, she was eager to sharpen her ability to see. And in fact, the instructor showed her within minutes that she was missing much of what she thought she could see. In one exercise, she was told to describe a photograph to a fellow participant, who drew the image based on her description. The photograph showed a cityscape with a bridge over a body of water. In the background, high-rise buildings framed a daytime sky. Easy, she thought. But when the exercise was over, the instructor said: "Raise your hand if you described the giant kitchen table and chairs on top of the bridge." The *what?* Incredulous, she looked at the photograph again and there, centered on top of the bridge, was a larger-than-life table and two chairs. She had not seen them because she hadn't expected to see them. Tables and chairs don't belong in a picture of a downtown bridge. But what doesn't belong, or what seems out of place, can be significant, perhaps essential, to our perception.

Fortunately, we can improve our visual intelligence and build upon our perceptual abilities in ways that can be helpful in our work and in our lives. Perception is related to the power of faith. The perceiving power of faith is your capacity to see the truth within a circumstance, similar to your ability to see what is significant in a photograph.

All perception is personal—subject to the limits of our training, our experience, and our bias. Abraham-Hicks argues that we are all perceptual beings with different vantage points:

It does not matter how much information is given—you cannot see beyond the vibrational limits of where you are standing. You cannot live or see or experience outside of your own individual beliefs.

In other words, everyone sees what they see. Not an earth-shattering revelation, of course, but an acknowledgment that involving others in looking can reveal more than we can see on our own. This is valuable knowledge that can lead to better meaning-making in life, as well as better decision-making.

Faith is your rightful spiritual power of perception, conviction, and expectancy. As you cultivate your perceiving power, what you *know* expands along with the realm of possibilities. What you expect to see grows as well. As Linda learned, we see what we expect to see. Open your mystical eyes for greater vision and insight.

Affirmation for Faith

By claiming the perceiving power of faith,
I expand my vision.
I look beneath the surface
Of my circumstances,
To that of me which is real,
And enduring, and whole.
By faith, I look beyond my circumstances

This Life Is Yours

To my whole life.
I believe in well-being as
The great possibility for each day.
Through faith, I cultivate a capacity
For positive, joyful expectancy.

IMAGINATION: CONCEPTION, VISION, EMBODIMENT

George R. R. Martin, author of *Game of Thrones*, tells of growing up within a five-block area of low-income housing in Bayonne, New Jersey. His family was so poor that they never went anywhere, and George longed to leave the confines of his hemmed-in community. When he discovered that he could travel anywhere he wanted in his imagination—even to other lands or other planets—he became a voracious reader of comic books and a writer of fanciful tales. When he found that other kids liked his imaginative stories, he sold them and gave dramatic readings about monsters to neighborhood kids for pennies. He went on to become a best-selling author, demonstrating that you can cultivate imagination regardless of the limitations seemingly imposed by your circumstances. You just have to conceive of a desired life experience, shape it by envisioning yourself there, and then live there in your imagination.

Does this mean that any flight of fancy can become part of your reality? Well, yes—in the sense that, as you conceive of a more glorious life experience and fill in its details by envisioning it, you positively alter your bio-chemistry. Moreover, you unleash universal creativity by engaging your head and heart, thinking and feeling, thus making the impossible possible.

What becomes possible in your imagination becomes possible in your experience. As you imagine yourself energized and inspired, you veer in that direction. As you envision that long-delayed vacation, you suspend contraindicated conditions like poor stamina or lack of funds. You interrupt what you consider reality in favor of a preferred altered reality, and you begin to embody that divine idea. You begin to benefit from the positive emotions stimulated by the creative possibility.

What possibility have you crossed off your list, certain that it could never be achieved? Try cultivating your ingenious power of imagination, because it can never become real if you never imagine it.

Affirmation for Imagination

Creating is natural to me.
Starting now, I aim to create the future
I have been dreaming about.
I rekindle my capacity to daydream,
To be the author of fantastical tales.
Imagining the life I have longed for,
I paint a visual picture of me in that life.

I live in that longed-for life so intently,
That I feel today the way I expect to feel
In that future.
I live in the state of imagination,
As I become the fulfillment of my dream.

UNDERSTANDING: COMPREHENSION, REALIZATION, INSIGHT

The role of understanding in your life can be dramatic. Whether you believe in a deity, a higher power, or universal intelligence, comprehending that you are more than your present condition is a key to realizing the truth of your wholeness. Realizing wholeness, you can challenge and change patterns of thought and emotion that have been running under the surface, ignored while symptoms have demanded all of your attention. As Eckhart Tolle observed: "To know yourself as the Being underneath the thinker, the stillness underneath the mental noise, the love and joy underneath the pain, is freedom, salvation, enlightenment."

Louise Hay, considered one of the founders of the self help movement, was a promoter of body, mind, and spirit healing. From her training in New Thought, Louise became known for connecting patterns of thought and feeling to health challenges. Her book *Heal Your Body* became a bible for countless followers. More recently, medical intuitive Mona Lisa Schulz coauthored *All Is Well* with Louise (2013), further developing their body, mind, and spirit approach to healing all manner of conditions. We recommend studying *All Is Well* to cultivate your magnificent capacity of understanding.

Likewise, Myrtle Fillmore's healing practices, mentioned in chapter 1, provide a helpful example of how to cultivate the power of understanding. At age forty-one, Myrtle fell prey to the tuberculosis that had ravaged her family in previous generations; she expected an early death. But then she heard a message that changed her life: "I am a child of God and therefore I do not inherit sickness." This led her to a breakthrough understanding that she belonged to an expansive universe grounded in wholeness. She internalized this spiritual realization and disconnected her experienced condition from her biological heritage, knowing in every fiber of her being that wholeness and wellness were natural and could be nurtured. Myrtle returned to physical health over a two-year period by attending to her body, mind, and spirit. She gained insight into the beliefs and emotional patterns that had prevented healing in the past, transforming her experience and her health. She lived to age eighty-six, serving others by sharing these practices.

We can all choose to suspend the intellect deliberately in favor of a more mystical pathway to understanding. Caroline Myss, renowned for her teachings about spirituality and human consciousness, proposes this in her book *Defy Gravity*:

> Achieving the impossible requires that you out-
> wit your voice of reason and access the whimsical
> part of your nature that inherently delights in the
> possibilities of the imagination . . . . [We] want
> to silence that reasoning, demanding, inquisitive
> intellect and fall into the breathless experience of
> inner trust.

Spiritual practices provide the kind of mystical pathways that lead to breakthroughs of understanding. We share many throughout this book. Choose a practice that gets you out of your head and into your heart. Linda loves kirtan and ecstatic dance. Alicia is all about coloring mandalas and chanting.

Affirmation for Understanding

Curiosity is natural to me.
I want to understand that of me
Which is real and true and enduring.
Although in the past I tried to figure out
Why unwanted things happened,
Today I am more interested in
How I can support wholeness and well-being.

My bright mind is capable of understanding
Habits of thought that have been unhelpful to me,
Capable as well of cultivating healthful habits of
   thought.
By my innate power of understanding,
I can go beyond conscious thought to
Spiritual, mystical reality where, in a state of awe,
I experience a direct and life-changing real-ization
Of my true nature—wholeness.

WILL:
CHOICE, COMMITMENT,
WILLINGNESS

"The willingness to accept responsibility for one's own life," Joan Didion tells us, "is the source from which self-respect springs." To cultivate your capacity of will—the power to choose and commit, the power to be willing—pause in your actions periodically, right where you are in the middle of your day, and remind yourself: *I am choosing this.* This simple declaration may be surprising in its consequences. It may lead you to smile or it may lead you to grimace. Either way, the awareness is a powerful stimulant.

Someone who had married happily after two unhappy marriages asked Linda how she and her husband had managed to remain together for forty years. Linda replied that she and her husband were likely in their third marriage as well! They had swirled in a few huge tempests over the years that had left them gasping and sputtering, reassessing, and making fresh agreements. After each crisis, however, they turned to each other and chose their marriage, saying: "This is where I choose to be. Every day when I wake up in your company, I choose my relationship with you." When she recognized that she had a choice, Linda recalls, she had no idea of the power she was unleashing. When she applied the same power of choice to other aspects of her life—her work, her friendships, her use of time, managing her money—she began to realize the full power of choice.

When you stand in an unwanted experience and claim the power of choice, you admit—like it or not—*I choose this*. If you do not like what you have chosen, or if you can see that you have chosen by default without exercising your power, there is no blame implied, only a next choice to be made. To be clear, we do not mean that you *choose* an illness or other unwanted condition; we mean that you choose how you will *experience* your circumstances. When Linda realized she had been choosing resentment in her marriage, she used the power of will to choose divine love and harmony instead.

When you choose consciously, you live by intention and further a growing awareness of your divine identity. It may be disconcerting when you recognize that, by choosing one thing, you deselect other options. But by agreeing to walk this one way, you make a commitment—perhaps only for a time, but certainly for now.

Like the flash of insight it truly is, the power of choice shifts you into the present moment, which is where power resides. No power exists in the past. No power exists in the future. Power lies in the present moment of awareness. You choose now. If you realize this in an unwanted moment, you can reclaim your rightful power to choose anew. And to be willing to walk that way.

Affirmation for Will

Whether or not I notice in any moment,
I am a choice-maker.
By the self-determining power of will,
I choose my attitude and outlook.
I choose how to respond to the demand
Of any moment's circumstances.
I declare with the full force of will,
I am not helpless. I never have been.
I choose the path ahead.
Will it be joyful or stressful? Easy or hard?
Choosing as best I can each day,
I am committed to great demonstrations
Of well-being that are possible for me.
On days when it seems too hard, too daunting,
To choose well-being,

On those days,
I am willing.

ZEAL:
ENTHUSIASM, AUDACITY, DEVOTION

"Zeal," Charles Fillmore tells us, "is the inward fire of the soul that urges [us] onward . . . the affirmative impulse of existence." In short, zeal is the command to go forward. Enthusiasm is the aspect of zeal that stems from your desires. You are *drawn* to the light; it begins with a flicker, a stirring in your stomach that is hard to ignore and keeps you awake at night.

Toddler Alicia used to laugh as she ran fearlessly into the ocean, worrying her parents, who had to grab her before the water surged over her head. Although Alicia today describes herself as cautious and hesitant, she can point to particular flashes of boldness when she changed her life by saying "yes!" In her early twenties, she moved to Chicago with no real plan other than visions of doing local theater and open-mic nights with the hope of being discovered. But those dreams quickly lost their glamor and she felt aimless.

In conversations with her family over the holidays, Alicia explored her vision for meaningful work. She felt passionate about helping others learn and was enthusiastic about working with children with special needs. She headed back to Chicago for the New Year with a new attitude and almost immediately found an open teaching-assistant position in a therapeutic day school for individuals with autism spectrum disorder that just seemed to shout: This is the one! Her enthusiasm was leading her in a completely different direction than she had envisioned, but she knew immediately that she was making a choice that aligned with her heart's calling. In every aspect of the work, she found a new lesson and a new opportunity to grow. She thrived as she made connections with her students, even during trying circumstances. Working at the school taught her about being in the present moment, about being her authentic self, and about the joy of fulfilling her purpose.

This was a time of maturing and clarity for Alicia—a time when she discovered that she had gifts to share with the world. As she came to recognize the light in herself, she saw it reflected everywhere. Her choices were affirmed and her relationships evolved. She didn't change; she just became more of her true self. She became bolder—more audacious. Audacity is, in fact, the aspect of zeal that proclaims: I am the Light! Linda defines it as "uncommon valor in the midst of common human circumstances" (*Divine Audacity*). By being audacious, Alicia became more in tune with her surroundings and more able to take action.

Devotion is the aspect of zeal that represents fulfillment. When you are able to do something with your life that is meaningful and wholly gratifying, you make

This Life Is Yours

the choice to show up. Alicia was completely dedicated to her students and knew that her presence did make a difference. So don't ignore your passions; explore them. See what opportunities they may hold for you. Dare to discover your zealous self. It is alive, and ready to live boldly.

Affirmation for Zeal

Enthusiasm is natural to me.
It is not always visible to others.
It doesn't require me to act like a giddy teenager.
Sometimes it is a flicker that builds into a fire,
A fire in the belly.
I claim divine audacity, my bold spiritual nature
By which I am daring and fully visible.
I am devoted to being good to myself,
Good to others, and good to the world
   around me.
My presence matters.
I do not shy away. I show up. I am zeal.

POWER:
CONCENTRATION, SELF-MASTERY, AUTHORITY

When her aging father was hospitalized after a stroke, Linda heard fear in his voice over the telephone. Her thoughts began leaping from stroke to death, from having her father to losing him. Then she paused and breathed into her power center. She immediately became aware of her dominant intention in that moment, which was to support her father rather than focus on her own experience. She withdrew her attention from frightening thoughts and redirected it to the power she had practiced—the power of self-mastery.

Self-mastery is an aspect of spiritual power, an innate capacity to guide your thoughts, words, and actions in spiritual integrity. Self-mastery can be cultivated. You can become proficient at pivoting your awareness away from reactive thoughts and feelings, and focusing attention instead on how to respond with spiritual power in the moment.

You may have been conditioned to think that you cannot trust your own thoughts. Can you recall times when your reaction in a moment of trouble only inflamed the situation? Have you regretted words that flew out of your mouth when you were provoked or decisions you made out of spite? Have you felt the dissonance between consuming worry over a loved one's well-being and your sure knowledge of their divine identity? These entirely human reactions have become the stuff of sitcoms and docudramas simply because they are reactions to which everyone can relate. But just because it's a natural response to strike first when you feel threatened or to lash out when you feel hurt doesn't make it a best practice. On the other hand, neither is it a best practice to hold your tongue in the face of injustice, to cower in the presence of a bully, or to presume your loved one is only human. These situations require you to invoke your spiritual power.

Your spiritual power resides in your ability to concentrate attention on what is most important, what is right in front of you, what is necessary in the moment. By means of spiritual power, you become master of your own mind. You are able to tame wild streams of thought; you know when to speak up and when to shut up. When you do speak, you speak with spiritual authority, which means that you declare only what you know is true, clarifying, and helpful.

As Linda ministered to her father, she drew on this power. She reassured him when he felt fear. She relied on her capacity to know his wholeness, even in the face of his illness. Her brain slowed and ceased its constant flurry of contradictory thoughts. She was able to move beyond her father's physical condition and focus on his positive outlook, his corny sense of humor, and his eagerness to connect with his caregivers. "Everything can be taken from a man but one thing," Victor Frankl assures us, "the last of the human freedoms—to choose one's attitude in any given set of circumstances, to choose one's own way" (*Man's Search for Meaning*). This is the power of self-mastery.

Affirmation for Power

I am the commander of my mind.
Like a laser beam of light that cuts through steel,
I concentrate attention on what is most important
Right now.
For all that is unfinished or uncertain,
Spiritual power is required.
I am master of my mind and my mood.
I practice self-mastery, knowing
When to speak up and when to shut up.
When I do speak, I declare what is true.
What is clarifying.
What is helpful.
I am a demonstration of spiritual power.

LOVE:
MAGNETISM, HARMONY, UNITY

Amy Pence-Brown was not sure what type of response she would get when she stopped in the middle of a large crowd in Boise, Idaho, to shed her clothes and reveal her forty-year-old body in a black bikini. Blindfolded, she stood with a sign at her feet that read: "I'm standing for anyone who has struggled with a self-esteem issue like me, because all bodies are valuable." She asked for the crowd to support her social experiment by drawing hearts on her body as she stood frozen and vulnerable. Amy, who had spent many years as a body-positive activist and artist, could not have imagined the ripple effect of this one small act as, one by one, people came and covered her body in hearts and words of affirmation. She had set out to spread a message of love and acceptance for all bodies, but found herself at the forefront of a movement that gained global attention through a viral video that has been viewed over 200 million times. "I finally realized it wasn't me that needed fixing or changing," she marveled. "It was society."

What inspires us about Amy's story is that she had already made the decision long before to be at peace with her own body. Her purpose that day was to stand in self-love so that others could allow themselves to do that as well. Many body-positive advocates are labeled as radical, because society just cannot wrap its head around someone in a larger body being truly comfortable in the skin they are in. It makes us uncomfortable and prompts us to come to terms with our own insecurities. Poet Nayyirah Waheed expresses the power of these societal inhibitions perfectly:

And I said to my body, softly, "I want to be
    your friend."
It took a long breath and replied,
    "I've been waiting my whole life for this."

Love is magnetic. Have you ever witnessed a marriage proposal in a public place? Everyone stops what they are doing and draws attention to the couple, and you can feel the love in the air. Love feels incredible, and we always want more of it. The love between that one couple magnifies the love within everyone viewing their special moment. Love harmonizes us. It looks good on us—especially self-love. Make an agreement to be compassionate and appreciative of your body temple. We recommend meditations that focus on where the energy is in your body. Visualize that energy as love pouring through the parts of your body that need it most.

Love unifies us. It spreads effortlessly and connects us. How many others do you think were walking around that day feeling uncomfortable in their own skin, thinking that they could never do what Amy was doing? How important the power of love is, that we see ourselves reflected in others. In fact, spiritually, love allows us to see no "other."

Amy is one example of how love attracts, unifies, and harmonizes. She brought awareness and acceptance to a large audience and reconciled the peace within herself. You, too, can cultivate a love like that. It is not radical to love yourself. In fact, it should be mandatory. Just as mothers and fathers strive to set positive examples for their children, you must live as the love you are. You have always known you are more than your body, but somewhere on your journey you may have allowed others' criticism, self-doubt, and media-mandated standards to be the judge of your physical beauty. Instead, make love the new standard. The world is craving it.

Affirmation for Love

Love is magnetic.
My desire is to be in the state of love.
No matter today's challenges,
Love is in the heart of me.
I look to love, my harmonizing power,
To integrate my thoughts and emotions,
My beliefs and experiences.
In the state of love, I know that I am one
With you, with life, within myself.
By the magnetizing, harmonizing, and
Unifying power of love,
I radically, unabashedly, wholeheartedly
Love.

WISDOM:
JUDGMENT, DISCERNMENT,
INTUITION

"Everything you'll ever need to know is within you,"
Dan Millman assures us. "The secrets of the universe are
imprinted on the cells of your body." And the decisions
you make every day rely upon this inner wisdom, whether
or not you recognize your own power. You judge, you
weigh, you evaluate options. You study, you talk things
over, you meditate to discern a sense of direction. You
dream, you get a bright idea, and suddenly you know the
way to proceed. Wisdom is yours. Trust it.

Alicia learned to trust her inner wisdom after receiving a devastating diagnosis of systemic lupus and fibromyalgia. At first, she frantically attempted to comprehend her medical condition, but blogs, online support forums, holistic recommendations, and the well-meaning advice of family and friends overwhelmed her. She felt defeated by the rheumatologist's insistence that she would be managing her symptoms for the rest of her life. She fell prey to fears of what would happen to her body and began to grieve for the life she was not yet living. She wanted to paste a fearless smile on her face, but the unknown felt beyond terrifying to her. Her prescribed medications left her feeling so sick that she couldn't function, so she resigned from her job and moved into her parents' home, resolving to dedicate the next few years of her life to holistic healing and a detoxification program.

As Alicia discovered, following the direction of inner wisdom is not a once-and-done proposition. Every day required her to rely on the power of wisdom for every next decision. After being on a holistic program for almost two years, she still wavered between feeling just okay and being mostly exhausted. The protocols were designed to stimulate continuous detoxification, but she still didn't seem to be making progress. Then one morning, as she prepared her weekly array of an extraordinary number of supplements, she asked herself why she was taking each one. She decided to follow her inner wisdom and start listening to her body. She discontinued one supplement, only to learn later that her body had not been processing it. At this critical decision point, she chose the power of judgment.

Your body knows what you need. When confronted with a crisis, assess your own unique needs and utilize the power of discernment to reveal hidden truths by asking: "Is this true for me?" You owe it to yourself to be a searcher, not just a researcher. We have years of collective experience in applying wisdom to dietary regimens. Maybe you have, too. Just because someone you know has had great success following a keto diet does not mean that it will benefit you. An elimination diet is a great way to gain insight into how certain foods affect your health, but the forced rigidity of following any certain protocol can have negative effects. You may be sensitive to a food that you are consuming in large amounts because it is on an "okay" list. Trust in the power of wisdom that validates your individual experience. Learn to become a vigilant student of your inner wisdom's teachings. As spiritual teacher Ram Dass advises: "The spiritual journey is individual, highly personal. Listen to your own truth."

Affirmation for Wisdom

Everything I need to know is within me.
Wisdom is my name.
My lists of plusses and minuses,
Pros and cons, and this-or-thats

Are tempered by the whisper of wisdom.
I judge only what is right for me.
I rely upon the wisdom in my body,
A nonphysical but sensed intelligence.
I trust my gut.
I am intuitive.
In this moment, I know my next step.
Next moment? I will know my next step.

ORDER:
ORGANIZATION, ADJUSTMENT, EVOLUTION

Alicia had always loved music, and singing was an important part of her identity. She turned thirty the day before the predicted end of the world according to the Mayan calendar—two apocalyptic events! And then, in the midst of the holiday frenzy, another devastating event struck. Her music died. On the morning of Christmas Eve, she woke up voiceless. Rather than singing *O Holy Night* at the church candlelight service, it looked as if it would be a silent night for her. In fact, a tiny tear was discovered in her vocal folds that would keep her from singing for almost two years. When she did start singing again, her confidence in her vocal abilities, built up over years of training, was gone. Her own voice sounded foreign to her. When, in the middle of a performance, she had a panic attack, Alicia realized in that moment that her need for perfection had become debilitating. Losing her voice was like losing herself.

The loss of her voice prompted Alicia to change her focus—to pivot—to using her creative talent in different ways. She began by working with toddlers at church. She learned to find great joy watching the children move through the world the way they wanted to, questioning and exploring and creating. Then she moved to the middle-school classroom, where she felt as if she had found her tribe. These blossoming adults taught her how to thrive in the unknown and she felt spiritually fed by them. She was creating, and the vulnerability implicit in all of that felt affirming. She was forging a new path without rigidity. She was playing!

Before this change in focus, Alicia had viewed order as regimenting and confining. Her goals as a singer had pushed her toward a quest for perfection that often took the fun out of performing. She felt as if she had to be perfect. But when she began working with children and learned how to play and have fun again, she gained a deeper understanding of order that allowed her to appreciate its adaptive power. When she lost her voice, Alicia felt as if she had lost her identity. But by changing her focus, she has, in fact, discovered more of her true self. She sees herself now as a young child playing with blocks—building and rebuilding, evolving. She has learned that the pieces of ourselves that we hold dear never break; they just transform before our eyes. By accepting the adaptive power of order and pivoting toward compatible passions and possibilities, she gained the kind of flexibility that never imposes a rigid set of prescriptions, but rather allows us to redirect our goals for greater fulfillment. TV personality Oprah Winfrey puts it this way:

Do the one thing you think you cannot do. Fail at it. Try again. Do better the second time. The only people who never tumble are those who never mount the high wire. This is your moment. Own it.

Affirmation for Order

Everyone has their own order and rhythm.
I have mine.
It may not be obvious to anyone else,
But I rely upon the power of organization
In my mind, which shows in my actions.
Not only am I organized, I am flexible.
When conditions are not ideal,
I adjust my thoughts and behaviors
For maximum support.
Order is never imposed upon me.
I claim and celebrate my power of order.

I am the very pulse of life-affirming order.
I dance down the road,
Evolving with every step.

STRENGTH:
STABILITY, COURAGE, TENACITY

The synthetic opioid fentanyl has been implicated in a shocking 45-percent increase in drug-overdose deaths in a single year, accounting for more than 70,000 deaths in 2016 alone. In 2017, our young cousin Tyler died from an overdose of heroin laced with fentanyl. He was twenty-two years old. For several months after Tyler's death, his mother, Sally, determinedly pressed her local law enforcement professionals to prosecute the drug dealer who had sold her son the lethal mix of drugs. A full year after Tyler's death, she learned the case had been dropped for insufficient evidence.

Unless you are a parent who has lost a child to addiction, you can hardly imagine Sally's feelings—disbelief that justice was not served; worry that others would have access to lethal drugs through the same dealer; sorrow about not having been able to prevent her son's addiction or his death; relentless grief. In fact, Sally will never be the person she was before Tyler's death. But the one thing she possesses that will guide her toward who she is becoming is spiritual strength—an innate power of uncommon stability, courage, and tenacity. After Tyler's death, Sally learned how to draw upon that strength and lead from it.

Sally has pivoted. She has committed herself to shining a light on the epidemic of drug abuse in her community. Fueled by grief and determination, and in her son's memory, she has become a lifeline to all who are touched by the tragedy of drug addiction. She walks the streets at night to locate kids who have checked themselves out of rehab. She holds the weeping parents of children who have overdosed. She arranges transportation to rehab facilities. She advocates for the vulnerable in public as well as in private. She established a scholarship fund for current and future students in her son's high school to continue their education or help them with detox and rehab. In short, Sally is a living demonstration of spiritual strength. After the unimaginable tragedy of Tyler's death exploded what had seemed an ordinary and predicable life, she used the stabilizing power of her spiritual strength to become an uncommon force for positive support. She drew from her inner courage to speak out and reach out to those in need of courage, lending her tenacious spirit to others in their desperation.

Like Sally, you may be in the middle of a destabilizing life circumstance. You may feel discouraged, bereft, or desperate. But you are not finished, friend. You may need a lifeline—someone like Sally—to assist you, but you have the same spiritual strength within you that Sally tapped into. You have it because you are, like Sally, like all of us, a spiritual being. Your true nature is wholeness—spiritual strength included.

Affirmation for Strength

Although I may have many reasons
To give up in discouragement,
I am not finished. I am strong.
Spiritual strength is my name.
When conditions threaten to destabilize me,
I stand steady and stable.
I steady myself in what is most important.
I uncover uncommon courage to speak
Words of truth and challenge where needed.
Courageously, I rise out of bed
On days I would rather skip.
I keep going. I am tenacious.
I persist.
I am strong.

RELEASE:
CLEANSING, RENUNCIATION, REPENTANCE

Who among us manages to gain some years without accumulating weight? Not physical weight, but rather all the weighty thoughts we absorb in our earliest years, reinforced by experience and morphed into solidified beliefs about ourselves and what is or is not possible for us. Like all human beings, you have probably collected these beliefs throughout your lifetime. Many of them may have proven constructive over time, but many others may have slowed your steps or chained you to seeming limitation.

Our friend Birdie inspires us. Like most of us, she has collected her share of helpful, as well as unhelpful, beliefs along her life's journey. She became particularly aware of them about a year ago when she fell and sprained her ankle. That ankle sprain, however, became more than a minor inconvenience when it was discovered that a previously undiagnosed congenital problem with her spine had led to her fall. The risk of another fall was severe enough that Birdie found herself confined to a wheelchair for several months, with no guarantee against future falls. Birdie was faced with keeping up with her responsibilities at work and at home—from her wheelchair. More significant for Birdie, however, was her state of mind. A student of New Thought for many years, she had grown in spiritual understanding. Yet she, like so many others visited by unwanted circumstances, felt crippled less by her physical condition than by limiting, self-condemning thoughts and beliefs.

But Birdie relishes a challenge. She confronted those thoughts and beliefs and activated her amazing spiritual power of release. She drew on her innate ability to cleanse her mind of nonproductive thoughts, to renounce untrue beliefs, and to pivot her mind in the direction of constructive meaning-making. She used the cleansing power of release to breathe out unhelpful thoughts as she became aware of them. And there were plenty. To make matters worse, Birdie's struggle was complicated by well-meaning others who chimed in with their own beliefs: "The universe is trying to teach you something." "God is telling you to slow down." "You will gain spiritual strength from this experience." This is what we lovingly call metaphysical malpractice!

But Birdie had the wisdom to pivot. She recognized her challenges as an opportunity to renounce false beliefs that had been operating beneath the surface for many years. She triumphed by saying "no" to these beliefs—gently yet emphatically. "No, God is not a cruel schoolteacher." "No, I did not somehow bring this on myself." "No, this is not a test of my endurance and self-sufficiency." "No, I cannot get through this alone." To paraphrase Emmet Fox, she starved these negative beliefs out of existence by refusing to feed them with the attention upon which they live (*Find and Use Your Inner Power*).

Birdie's pivot became apparent as she welcomed support along her way, as the quality of her thoughts improved, as she allowed herself to feel fully, and as she prayed. She also translated her own experience into showing more compassion for others. She did what she could, in a wheelchair, until the day came when she could gratefully stand on her own two feet again.

Affirmation for Release

Let me not be captivated by scrolling thoughts
On autopilot.
I am fully able to know the difference
Between helpful and unhelpful thinking.
I activate my innate power of release
To gently slough off unhelpful,
Nonproductive thoughts.
I am fully able to know the difference
Between truth and untruth.
I renounce untrue patterns of thinking,
Clearing my mind so that my heart
Can know the truth.

LIFE:
ANIMATION, VITALITY, PRESENCE

Life is the animating power, the very flow of energy in and through our bodies. It also encompasses the flow of our shared experiences that transform self-understanding. Alicia remembers a profound experience of the power of life when she was on tour in Germany with the Young Americans, a global not-for-profit performing group teaching music workshops. The cast was booked to lead a performance workshop at a juvenile correctional facility. They were herded, wide-eyed and silent, onto a bus for the short ride to the prison. The reality of their destination did not set in, however, until they were patted down and heard the gates lock behind them. Nothing she had experienced in her performing career or her travels to ten different countries could have prepared Alicia for this experience.

Music filled the gymnasium as a swarm of young men between eighteen and twenty-five plowed through the doors and paraded around them in matching shirts and pants. It felt like a junior-high dance at first, with everyone awkwardly waiting for someone to start dancing. Some of the men grouped together against the walls and stared blankly back at the cast. Then, as if a switch had been thrown, they all started mingling and dancing in a circle with the cast. By the end of that first night, they were all practicing dance steps, laughing, and encouraging the few who were still hanging back to join in. Everyone ate dinner together at long tables and the young men shared stories of how they had ended up in prison, and how they missed their families and their homes. It was raw, painful, and powerful. Then the guards lined the inmates up and returned them to their cells for the night.

The next day, the doors to the gymnasium flew open and the young men came bounding in, eyes bright, alert and ready to go. The cast started by teaching them choreography to a medley from *The Lion King* that played on the drumbeat as the heartbeat—the life force that vitalizes our experiences and connections, and is the power of life in each and every moment. As Alicia stood in the front, facing everyone as she sang, she saw a gymnasium filled, wall-to-wall, with slow, powerful, unified movement. These men, who could have been hardened by their experiences, were singing their hearts out, standing tall with pride, some crying and holding on to each other. It is an image she will never forget. The power of life—the power of vitality—ran deep in these young men, who let down their guard to feel the full force of their inner drive. On the final day of the visit, the inmates joined with the cast to perform for the prison staff and what felt like an entire town who had shown up out of curiosity. The performance was a rainbow of colors and emotions that ended in the longest standing ovation Alicia had ever witnessed. The audience threw flowers while the inmates exchanged hugs with the cast, until the guards signaled and they lined up single file to return to their cells—still singing.

Life is what you make of it. Let an awakened sense of this fill you in this present moment. Whether in the prison of your mind or a literal prison, breathe new life into what you are experiencing. Close your eyes and feel the energy of life coursing through your body. Revel in the great potential within you, the inner resources that you can cultivate and draw upon for healing.

Affirmation for Life

I am in tune with the animating power of life.
Every part of me, material and spiritual,
Is thrumming with life.
I feel for flowing, pulsing, thrilling ideas
And I give life to them.
I am running in life-producing,
Life-sustaining, and life-enhancing circles.
Everything I give life to, lives!
I am a vital presence.
The life I am contributes. Blesses.
Encourages. Inspires.

CHAPTER 5

The Impact of Intentional Action

My advice to other disabled people would be, concentrate on things your disability doesn't prevent you doing well, and don't regret the things it interferes with. Don't be disabled in spirit as well as physically.

—Stephen Hawking, *New York Times* Interview

When the actions you take each day are conscious and intentional, you develop habits that foster your identity as a whole being. Whatever deepens self-realization; whatever shifts awareness from something wrong to something wonderful; whatever furthers your longing and its fulfillment; whatever challenges your unchallenged beliefs; whatever sends shivers down your spine; whatever shakes your foundation; whatever provokes and disturbs you; whatever leads you onto an unfamiliar path—act intentionally from these things.

In this chapter, we will explore daily practices that can help you develop your capacity for intentional action and anchor you in wholeness. Select a variety of these practices that are manageable for you in your own circumstances, focusing on those you believe you most need. Don't try to do everything; just do one thing each day for your spiritual well-being. These efforts will strengthen your mental, emotional, and biological well-being as well.

THE FIFTEEN-MINUTE BREAK

Do you think your life is too far off-track to believe in your own wholeness? Are you convinced that you have been doing your best to cope with multiple conditions, a complex disease, or emotional drain from unending relationship issues? Have you been facing challenges for so long that you have become discouraged, or despondent, or consigned to live in perpetual stress? If you answer "yes" to any of these questions, stress is likely too small a word for what you may be feeling. Stress is cumulative; once it takes root, it gains momentum and magnitude, like a snowball rolling down a hill. If you have ever found yourself saying "Just one thing on top of another" or "If one more thing goes wrong, I will break," chances are you have experienced this phenomenon.

It can seem impossible, when you are steeped in stress, to accept a message of wholeness—that nothing can be missing, wrong, or broken about you. This message seems to run contrary to your current experience. You certainly can justify and attest to plenty of evidence for what appears lacking, and we are not suggesting that you ignore or discount your very real experience. But continuing to spin in the swirl of your present stress just keeps you stuck right where you are. Instead, try choosing one practice from this book that you believe you can do every day for fifteen minutes to interrupt the relentless stress—like pressing a pause button while watching a video or taking a restroom break. These few minutes of relief can help break the cycle of stress and interrupt the momentum of that snowball. Day by day, the effects of these interruptions will build incrementally, providing longer-lasting relief. A small investment each day can lead to big improvements in your ability to cope, in your optimism and hope, and ultimately in your agreement with wholeness as the truth about you.

Allopathic medicine is fast catching on to what holistic medicine has proclaimed all along—that healing involves body, mind, and spirit. Think of the good that could come from devoting as much time and effort to spiritual practices as we devote to medical treatment. It could make all the difference. In *How to Pray without Talking to God*, Linda recommends writing your own prayers for healing. Think of them as spiritual prescriptions and follow them as carefully as you follow your medical prescriptions. Take fifteen minutes each day to step away from circumstances as they are and to be in touch with a broader sense of self.

SPIRITUAL PRACTICES A TO Z

The practices given below will support you in knowing unconditional wholeness and well-being. None of them require adherence to a particular theology or tradition. Most can be performed in under fifteen minutes. Choose one or two to start, and feel the stressors in your life begin to fade.

Affirmation

Release and affirmation, practiced together, make a potent tool for healing. You can build a healthy body with your heartfelt words of affirmation. Instead of subjecting your body to weak or sick thoughts, speak words of strength and health—and keep at it. Don't worry about what has been, Charles Fillmore tells us. "Clear out of your mind all rubbish about disease and you will find that none has any lodgment in your body" (*Atom-Smashing Power of Mind*).

Focus on your body—a particular location, an organ system, or your whole body. Prepare for the powerful effects of these affirmations by choosing a time and place that support reflection and meditation. You can recite these statements of release, or write your own.

- Power and strength are my spiritual capacities; therefore I refuse to believe in helplessness and weakness.

- I refuse to be in bondage to a false idea of susceptibility to disease.

- I release beliefs accumulated through the years that limit my potential health and vigorous living.

- I let go of unhelpful thoughts that cause me to feel worried about my health or to reduce my options for living fully.

- I deny any truth to the collective-consciousness agreement about disease, deterioration, or diminishment of my body's capacity to support life through the years.

- I say an absolute "No!" to another moment lived within the limits of my perceived incapacities.

Use these statements to affirm your power and wholeness, or write your own:

- I am divine, one with the enlivening power of life.

- My identity is divine; therefore I shine the light of perfect wholeness into my body and my daily living.

- Infinite wisdom is ever-present; therefore I can trust my deepest intuition.

- Divine love is my true nature; therefore I can live in harmony with my life and with all of life.

- Eternal life is the irrepressible vitality and flow from which I give life to my intentions.

- By my rightful power of divine order, I insert order and adjust to changing conditions with spiritual power.

- By my spiritual power of strength, I am stable, courageous, and tenacious in all things.

- By the light of divine power, I think, say, and do all that supports health and well-being as the author of my life.

- By the light of spiritual faith and imagination,
  I continually envision and walk toward greater
  capacities in mind and body.

Breath

Sitting or standing in as stable a posture as possible, breathe with your whole body. Raise your arms while inhaling and lower them as you exhale. Bend forward while exhaling and rise up while inhaling. Explore micromovements along with your in-and-out breaths. Focus on feeling alive as you move and breathe. Generate feelings of appreciation for every sensation and ability. Whenever you become aware that your mind has wandered, return your focus to breathing consciously.

A variety of breathing practices, or *pranayama* (meaning "control of the breath"), are found in yoga. For example, *ujjayi* is slow, deep breathing. Draw breath up from the back of your throat, which should sound like a reverse sigh. Exhale the same way, slowly and deeply, until your lungs are deflated. This practice is usually done sitting cross-legged on the floor or in a seated meditation pose.

Another yoga technique, known as *nadi shodana*, uses ujjayi with alternate-nostril breathing. Raise one hand to your face so that your thumb lies next to your nose on one side and your fourth and fifth fingers lie on the opposite side. Bend the middle two fingers out of the way. Cover one nostril with your thumb while inhaling slowly and deeply. If possible, pause for a few seconds before releasing your thumb. Then cover your other nostril with your fourth and fifth fingers as you exhale slowly. Repeat, starting with the nostril from which you just exhaled. It may take several breaths for you to get into a meditative rhythm. Once you do, breathe easily as your mind quiets.

Creativity

Devote a period each day to a hobby or artistic expression. If you already engage in such a practice, stimulate creativity by using your nondominant hand, which elevates brain function and increases hand-eye coordination. This practice requires your full attention, so it interrupts stressful and worrisome patterns of thought.

Devotion

Read and reflect on your favorite inspirational literature. If you follow a particular religious tradition, read your scriptures. Many traditions offer daily devotional messages, including Unity's *Daily Word*, which is available by subscription in print or digital form. Several contemporary self-help authors and teachers offer daily messages that are inspiring without referencing religion. Choose one that supports you, and build a simple practice of devoting a little time each day to reading and reflecting. Try lifting a quotation or a meaningful sentence from your reading and writing it in your journal.

Eat Mindfully

Mindful eating is a simple practice you can incorporate into your daily routine. Choose one meal or snack period to devote to the practice. Set your table. Silence your phone, television, and electronic devices. Set aside your reading material. Check that you have everything you need on and around your table, including condiments and beverages, utensils and supplements. Begin with a moment of conscious breathing and an attitude of appreciation. Then eat; simply eat. Notice the fragrance, texture, and taste of each morsel. Keep your mind present to every bite, savoring and enjoying it.

Forgiveness

Forgiveness entails shifting from a negative to a neutral emotion. When you are aware of an issue you would like to feel better about, this method, called *The Sedona Method*, is a helpful starting practice. Simply ask yourself these three questions:

- Can I let this feeling go?

- Will I let this feeling go?

- When will I be ready to let this feeling go?

Trust your first response. Avoid over-thinking. Continue asking these questions, noticing your responses and deepening your inquiry until you gain insight and the ability to release. You will know when you shift, because you will feel peaceful and nonreactive when you think about the issue. You can learn more about this simple yet powerful practice at *sedona.com*.

Gratitude

No practice is more valuable than gratitude. In fact, gratitude is essential for healing. It is often the hardest attitude to hold when we do not feel well, yet it helps us feel better. A gratitude practice can be as simple as recalling positive moments at the close of your day. Pause before a meal to express gratitude. Consciously thank the people around you every day. Prepare for a day of gratitude as you wake, appreciating your comfortable pillow or the sun streaming in through your window. Incorporate inspirational quotes into your decor, or tag your mirrors with messages of thanks.

Abraham-Hicks suggests a practice called a "rampage of appreciation." This practice is most helpful when it's hard to feel thankful. Consciously bring to mind every little thing you can authentically feel thankful about in the moment. Every little thing. For example, when you are unable to get out of bed, appreciate the flow of breath in your body and each of your body parts in turn. Flood your mind and heart with gratitude so that there is no room left for anything but appreciation.

Heart Opening

Any meditation that focuses attention on your heart will open it. HeartMath, a science-based practice for calming and balancing thoughts and feelings, is one such practice (see *heartmath.com*).

For several minutes, breathe in and out softly while focusing attention on your heart. If it helps you to focus, place one or both hands over your heart while you breathe. Develop a gentle rhythm—several seconds in and several seconds out. All the while, imagine that your breath originates in your heart, arising there when you inhale and flowing from there as you exhale. Slow your breathing a little more with each breath, until you are relaxed and breathing deeply. Then bring to mind a memory of a moment in which you experienced pure love and appreciation. Remember minute details. Feel as if it is happening right now. Bask in this memory.

Imagination

Identify several household objects or items in your present environment to use for this practice—this can be as simple as a slotted serving spoon you see in a canister on your kitchen counter. Make up alternate uses for these items that can support you in feeling your best. For instance, this spoon can scoop out bones and gristle from soup stock, but it can also scoop out nonsense from your thinking brain, returning it to clarity. Or play like a child. Skip rope; throw jacks; play dodge ball; build a sandcastle; daydream; crawl around on all fours; sing silly songs; create your own language—you get the idea.

Japa Meditation

Japa meditation, widely practiced in Hinduism, involves repetition of a *mantra*, a Sanskrit term meaning "the thought behind sound." It is often performed by moving your fingers along a string of mala beads, reciting the mantra each time you move to the next bead. Mantras are usually affirmative, perhaps devotional, words or phrases. Although traditional japa meditation is performed using a Sanskrit mantra, the practice is easily adaptable to any language and culture. In fact, the Roman Catholic rosary resembles japa meditation.

Linda learned a Sanskrit mantra that she relies on for japa meditation: *Om Namo Bhagavate Vasudevaya*, which, loosely translated, means: "I bow to the powerful, compassionate light of the divine." Familiar English-language affirmations can also be used for japa meditation, including:

- Be still and know.

- I am enough.

- All is well.

- My heart is open.

- God is my source.

Kindness

Small kindnesses activate our love faculty, vibrationally connecting us with others. Micro-kindnesses are possible for everyone, regardless of our circumstances. For example, when someone you love comes to mind, pray for their well-being, send them a card, or call them. Write messages of appreciation for your caregivers, or tell them of your gratitude. Look for a name tag on store clerks and address them by name. Make a game of it, giving thought to how you can extend kindness each day.

Learning

Become selective about reading, choosing content that inspires curiosity and insight. In the same way, choose what you view on television and on electronic devices carefully. Gravitate toward topics of high value for you, like healing, living well, spirituality, and creativity.

Devote time to learning more about a subject that you have encountered. Nowadays, you can find all manner of instructional content online. You can even learn the basics of some spiritual practices this way, including EFT (Emotional Freedom Technique)—aka, tapping. Study the mystical teachings of your faith tradition, or quantum physics, or a creative discipline like pen-and-ink drawing. Devoting a small amount of time each day can lead to greater knowledge or skill, and thus to increased well-being.

Mindfulness

Unlike other forms of meditation, the aim of mindfulness is not to quiet the mind or achieve an ecstatic state. The aim of mindfulness is to observe the present moment, just as it is, without judging or avoiding. Through this practice, you can become skilled at recognizing the continuous mental chatter and the constant criticism that go on under the surface of your awareness. It sounds so simple, and it is. But it is not as easy as it sounds.

There is no right or wrong way to do this practice. However, it can have significant benefits over time. Jon Kabat-Zinn, creator of the Center for Mindfulness in Medicine, Health Care, and Society at the University of Massachusetts Medical School, wrote:

Mindfulness practice means that we commit fully in each moment to be present, inviting ourselves to interface with this moment in full awareness, with the intention to embody as best we can an orientation of calmness, mindfulness, and equanimity right here and right now.

To practice mindfulness meditation, merely sit and observe the present moment without trying to alter it. Notice sensations without judging them. For example, if you notice that your nose itches, just notice! If you notice your mind taking off from your itchy nose to wondering whether you are catching a cold, simply notice and return to the present moment. Do this again and again, noticing physical sensations, thoughts, and emotions.

Nature Connection

You can connect to the Earth's natural energy to support health and well-being through a practice called "earthing." If you are able to go outside, lie in a field, or walk a path in the woods, or dip your toes in a stream, or just sit in your backyard. By connecting yourself to nature, you become grounded and place yourself squarely in the here and now. Your feet are on the ground; you become calm and aware. Your body also absorbs vital nutrients outdoors.

Circumstances may prevent you from going outside, but you can always bring the outdoors inside. Symbols like stones and feathers can help with this, but you can also use your imagination to visualize yourself in the natural world. If you are sensitive to the sun, an infrared sauna is a healthful substitute that can provide the benefits of detoxification and relaxation. You can probably find one at your local spa or holistic clinic. You can create an earth-based altar or meditation table that features symbols of the elements like water fountains, candles, gemstones, and chimes. Or you can simply listen to recordings of nature sounds like waterfalls, ocean waves, and birdsong.

Om Chanting

The sound of *Om*—in some traditions, *Aum*—is the sound of oneness, the vibration of peace. Om is a primal mantra that links us with the source of all that we can ever imagine. Regular Om chanting has been shown to have subtle yet demonstrable benefits like improving health, boosting mental clarity, promoting emotional well-being, and increasing spiritual insight. Although there are many variations of it, the practice is as simple as vocalizing the syllable. You can incorporate it into your meditation or prayer practice by chanting for a period of five minutes or more. Beginning with pranayama or breath practice may be helpful.

Take in a deep yoga breath, then open your mouth wide and begin vocalizing "Ah." Slowly purse your lips, continuing passive exhalation as the sound changes to "Ooh." Close your lips and raise your tongue to the roof of your mouth as you finish exhaling with an extended "Mm." Pause if you can before inhaling and repeating. Experiment with lower as well as higher pitches on the scale, noticing the regions within your body that are stimulated by different frequencies. You can find instruction for Om chanting online, and opportunities for group Om chanting may be available in your community.

Prayer

If you are a follower of a faith tradition or spiritual path, practice your path's form of prayer or meditation. For some, prayer consists of praying with a partner once each week. Identify a friend who has agreed to join you in this practice for a specified number of weeks. Meet either by telephone or video-chat, or in person at an agreed time. Support each other as you take turns praying in the manner of your faith tradition, boosting your capacities of expectancy, vitality, and tenacity. If you do not relate to prayer, you can adapt this practice by calling a friend to exchange affirmations.

If you consider yourself spiritual, but are not religious, you may find value in affirmative prayer as taught by Unity. Affirmative prayer, simply put, turns your mind to what is most true by holding in your consciousness a statement of well-being and wholeness. When your mind is swimming in confusion, alternately hopeful and worried, affirmative prayer can cut through the confusion to assert mental order, leading to a spiritual realization of health, which in turn leads to calm, confident thought and action. "Prayer is not something you do to God or say to God, or a performance you put on for God," Eric Butterworth observes in *Discover the Power within You*. "It is, in silence, finding the point in you where God is Being being you." Myrtle Fillmore concurs: "Prayers aren't sent out at all! Sometimes that is our trouble. Where would we send our prayers? We should direct them to our minds and hearts and affairs."

Here are some affirmations you may choose to dwell on in prayer:

- God is health, the state of well-being that is natural to me regardless of my circumstances.

- God is wholeness; therefore I am whole and complete in every moment.

- God is life, an ever-flowing vitality independent of changing conditions. God is the life I am.

- My every thought of God-life builds strength, vigor, and power.

- Divine life is my life. Wholeness is my nature and well-being is my natural state of being.

A simple pattern for affirmative prayer begins with receptivity and openhearted willingness. At a time and in an environment of calm focus, recite your affirmation, then reflect on its meaning, seeking to understand it as a truth that can alter the way you think and act. Afterward, sit in a state of meditation for a few moments, letting the power of the truth take hold in ways that logic alone cannot accomplish. When you return to conscious thought, consider what actions you can take to live in realization of this truth. Always end by expressing appreciation. You may choose to write your reflections in a journal.

A sure sign of an effective prayer for healing is this: You go on with life. In other words, once you realize the truth of innate wholeness and well-being, you cease worrying about shifting conditions. A setback here or a new symptom there cannot shake you, because you are anchored in the truth that leads you to live well today, as well as you are able.

Quest—Become an Explorer

Another pathway to healing may seem counterintuitive. Instead of attempting to escape from swirling emotions, dive into them. Instead of avoiding disturbing circumstances, explore them. Linda was drawn to explore ancient ruins in the vast expanses of the Southwest, searching for remnants of invisible life within the visible remains of a culture. This kind of exploration can be a metaphor for an emotional and spiritual quest. Whether climbing ladders to cliff edges, or exploring underwater reefs, or spelunking, or skydiving into a rain forest, or rafting down the Nile, you can reach out to deep truths about the world and about yourself. Just choose your metaphor.

If these kinds of physical quests are beyond your means or capabilities, write in your journal, or converse with a friend, or sit in creative visualization. Allow a memory to surface. Follow it wherever it leads you, noticing the dual energies of curiosity and caution, daring and danger, along the way, all the while knowing you are safe. Whatever you remember is a relic of a distant past. Whatever you discover about the relationship of your past to your present is a gift of fresh perspective and understanding. Whatever meaning you assign to that perspective is an integrator, a harmonizing force that leaves you whole.

Rest

A brief period of intentional rest during typical waking hours may seem unrelated to other daily practices in this section. But whether you are in Spain for *siesta*, in Italy for *riposo*, or on your yoga mat for *yoga nidra*, napping is a healthful form of renewal. Intentionally signing off from the goings-on around you for a short time can be rejuvenating and life-enhancing. Unplug your devices, plug up your ears, darken your space, wrap your body to avoid the distraction of drafts, enter a resting pose, cover your eyes, and become still.

A word about *yoga nidra*. Yoga nidra is not actually napping. It is a practice that falls somewhere between napping and meditation, a state of restful awareness or deep relaxation. You can follow instructions for this practice on an app, or focus on each area of your body in turn, from your feet to your head, softening and relaxing.

Singing

There's a reason why James Corden's *Carpool Karaoke* goes viral, and why some of the most memorable movie scenes include characters in the unlikeliest circumstances breaking out in song. Singing makes us feel good. To be clear, singing releases feel-good chemicals in our bodies that elevate our mood, improve circulation, and strengthen our immune system. You can sing alone in the shower or while preparing a meal. You can sing and dance to music that you love in your own private karaoke. Choose music and lyrics that uplift and inspire you. Join a local choir, participate in kirtan, or gather a group of friends for Om chanting to experience the heightened effects of singing in community.

Tonglen

Tonglen is a beneficial spiritual practice for cultivating compassion that originated in Buddhism. The word itself means "giving and receiving." The practice starts with two basic acknowledgments: suffering exists, and it is possible to be free from suffering. In tonglen, rather than avoiding your own suffering or the suffering of others, you let it in, knowing full well that you are not attaching to it, but rather transforming it and sending back relief. It is a simple but profound practice for hearts committed to helping others and themselves. To help ourselves, we must help others.

Tonglen practice consists of four parts. To prepare yourself, sit in a chair you use for prayer, meditation, or reflection, or assume your preferred meditation pose.

- Begin with affirmations for opening your heart. Read a heart-opening prayer from your faith tradition; speak your intentions to draw out your compassionate heart; or read the tonglen affirmation given here.

- Breathing in and breathing out is a natural form of circulation, of receiving and giving. Breathe in sensations of heat, darkness, or heaviness, which represent suffering. Breathe out coolness, brightness, or weightlessness, which represent well-

This Life Is Yours

being. Continue breathing in and out until you have established a rhythm and are immersed in receiving and giving.

- Bring to mind someone you care about who is suffering. Name the suffering: pain, loneliness, inferiority, hopelessness. Breathe in that suffering, then breathe out with your mind fixed on sending out relief and well-being. You can do this with your own suffering, or open your heart in compassion, mercy, love, and kindness for another.

- Broaden your practice to include all others who are suffering. Continue breathing in their suffering, then breathing out relief and well-being. Send out compassion, mercy, love, and kindness.

For more about tonglen practice, go to *lionsroar.com* or *shambhala.com*.

Tonglen Affirmation

Suffering. Shame. Hardship.
I will not run from you.
I will feel you.
I will invite you in, as a guest, not an inhabitant.
Whether you are mine or someone else's,

You came to visit me.
I can be hospitable, but know this:
My whole heart can heal you.
You will leave here whole.

Unpractice

Discontinue an unhelpful, unfulfilling habit like consuming a daily adult beverage or watching the news just before bedtime. Notice how you feel when you no longer rely on this habit. Intentionally replace the habit with another, more life-enhancing option.

Visioning

For a period of twenty-one days or longer, devote ten or fifteen minutes a day to envisioning the life you want most. Write in your journal how you feel when you have what you most desire. Specifically, write about how it feels to wake up each morning knowing you are at your best. This practice is very helpful when you do not believe you have yet achieved all you want to achieve.

The key to this visioning practice is to be as broad as possible without being vague. For example, write about feeling happy in your graceful body rather than focusing on your hips and legs alone. Write about feeling flexible, energetic, and at ease as you walk through your neighborhood park. Or write about an ideal start-to-finish day as you imagine it can be. Draw pictures with words, choosing descriptive language. For example:

- I awaken refreshed after a restful night of sleep. Pausing before getting out of bed, I feel so grateful, delighted that my mind is clear, my heart is open, and I feel utterly ready for a new day. When I stand, I love feeling strong and stable, eager to get going.

- I love waking up feeling amazed that I get to do what I love, supporting people who are determined to live well. Every cell in my body feels most alive and joyful when I think about meeting with one person after another, listening deeply to their stories and championing their well-being. I feel giddy at the very thought of it.

Each day, begin with a blank journal page and write your entire vision. Some days, you may seem to be writing nothing new, but keep at it, putting language to your vision and feeling your way to the life you most want. This isn't about wishing for magical cures or solving all of life's problems. It's about being what you can be and want to be in the time ahead of you. As Linda wrote in *Divine Audacity*:

What can be, can be when I hold a potent idea while I feel now how I expect to feel when it is fulfilled. Thinking and feeling as one creative mind activity is a preposterously simple yet underutilized practice.

Writing

Write in your journal about feeling capable and masterful. Review recent experiences, noting your ability to respond positively, constructively, or intentionally. If you cannot recall any such experiences, make them up! Tell the story as you would want it to be, convincing yourself of your capability.

Several helpful books have been written about journal writing, including *Start Where You Are: A Journal for Self-Exploration* by Meera Lee Patel and, for deep inner exploration, *Writing Down Your Soul: How to Activate and Listen to the Extraordinary Voice Within* by Janet Conner.

X

What if X? Engaging your faculty of imagination, pose some "what if. . ." questions and make up answers to them that are outrageous, thrilling, unbelievable, implausible, and utterly desirable. Write them, speak them out loud, or share them with someone. This practice is especially effective when the questions are focused on your healing or your heart's desires. This practice works best if continued for at least twenty-one consecutive days.

Yoga

Yoga is a popular practice that benefits body, mind, and spirit. There are many types of yoga, each with its own protocols. If you want the stress-reducing, mood-improving, body-easing benefits of yoga, try restorative yoga, a kind of anti-calisthenics. This is the perfect practice for recovering physical flexibility without pain. In a restorative yoga session, you are guided to slow, gentle movements and postures supported by props like bolsters, blocks, and blankets that allow you to soften into a pose without strain. Once successfully in a pose, you hold it for five minutes or longer, softening and releasing muscle tension. The result is relaxed muscles, greater flexibility, and feelings of tranquility.

Try a simple forward bend. Sitting on the floor with your legs outstretched in front of you, fold your upper body down and stretch it out over your legs. If there is a gap between your torso and your legs when you bend forward, fill it with a bolster or as many rolled blankets as you need to get a stretch that feels good without strain. Fold into the pose, relaxing there for at least five minutes; more is better. The more you relax, the more your upper body will sink into the bolsters. Rest and make micro-movements to increase the stretch and heighten relaxation.

You can learn restorative yoga by attending a class, or by using instructional videos and images online at *gaia.com* or *yogajournal.com*.

Zoom In

For a period of time, practice wholehearted, single-minded living by zooming in on one interest, talent, or desire that motivates or excites you. Devote yourself to learning, redirecting your focus away from concerns about your circumstances. Enroll in a webinar, take classes at your local library, join a book club or study group, or learn a new language. Learn how to make your own soap or kombucha. Audition for a community chorus or the theater. When you concentrate your attention exclusively on something of high interest to you, you stimulate feel-good chemicals in your body that improve your energy and outlook.

CHAPTER 6

Embrace Your Whole Life

You may not always have a comfortable life and you will not always be able to solve all of the world's problems at once, but don't ever underestimate the importance you can have, because history has shown us that courage can be contagious and hope can take on a life of its own.

—Michelle Obama, Keynote Address at Young African Women Leaders' Forum

Once you activate your spiritual capacities by committing to intentional action, you begin to see yourself more clearly. You open to the whole of *you* and begin to craft a fullness of life that leads to feelings of well-being. You learn to respect and be responsive to your intuitive wisdom, out of which arise clues to your own innate capacities. By honoring your past, your feelings, your needs, and your ability to wait, you become better able to honor your wholeness and to embrace your whole life.

HONOR YOUR PAST

The past is a chameleon. Although certain facts can be chronicled—recorded in a birth certificate, documented in a census report, or reported in a newspaper article—facts as you remember them change with each telling of your story. In essence, you change your history every time you revisit it.

Memories are fluid and, as such, unreliable, inconsistent, and incomplete. Facts may remain facts, but memory is subjective. Psychology explains this phenomenon. Every time you revisit a memory, you tell a new story—one that comes from the full force of who you are today rather than who you were when you first lived that experience. In other words, today's you is different from yesterday's you! But if memory is so changeable and unreliable, what is its value and how can you honor your past in a way that fosters healing? You can start by seeking understanding or clarification about the things that have bothered you.

Memories are distinctive and often contradictory. You infer from them meaning unique to your personal story and your personal wounds. You may be clinging to a memory that carries weight for you, but pay attention when your memories are very different from those of your siblings or classmates, especially if you harbor resentment or if you believe something in your past prevents your living well today.

For example, Linda spent years longing for her mother's approval, feeling she was judgmental and impossible to please. But not everyone did. She and her siblings have very different memories of their childhood—almost as if they were growing up in different households. Linda healed many of her own issues by listening to the other voices from her past who gave her the gift of their unique perceptions. In fact, recounting different details of shared experiences promotes connection, which is another way to honor your past.

Genealogical research has become a form of popular entertainment, as evidenced by television shows like *Who Do You Think You Are?*, *Finding Your Roots*, and *Genealogy Roadshow*. Revelations about an ancestor's character and behavior often move us to tears. When we find a thread of similarity in an ancestor's story, or the reproduction of a family trait, or the sense of a common cause, we tend to be healed by the revelation. Whether your ancestor owned slaves, was an abolitionist, or was enslaved, you realize that your destiny flows from theirs. Whether they fought on the right or wrong side of the revolution, you claim them. You relate to their courage, their endurance, and their resilience. You connect with their creativity or work ethic. You come from them. You belong to them. You honor them.

As genealogy proves, unknown aspects of your history can still affect you. And it is equally true that you may *know* something about your past without having conscious memory of it. Psychoanalyst Christopher Bollas coined the phrase the "unthought known" to suggest what you have experienced, and therefore know, but have not thought about. The unthought known represents your early life experiences before you had words to describe them or the awareness to think about them. In cases where family secrets are harbored—especially traumatic secrets like questionable parentage, incest, or addictions—children can grow up with a sense of something important that is hidden or best not thought about, yet felt.

When you review your past and reflect on all that has shaped your present experience, if you become aware of an unthought known, you can trust that it is coming up so that you can inquire about it, resolve it, and heal it. Honor your memories and your impressions of the past.

Affirmation to Honor the Past

My present has been shaped by my past.
Memories come as gifts to my awareness.
I honor my memories even as I question them,
Searching for the truth in them.
I remain curious and open about my history,
About the forces and faces that connect me
To the world beyond my borders.
Folding in, integrating, harmonizing
Everything I remember and learn about my past,
I heal.

HONOR YOUR FEELINGS

Memories and feelings are related. Both can arise seemingly out of nowhere; both can be hard to trace or define; both can be misleading. Feelings flow from memories, whether clear and in context or vague and unattached to a particular circumstance. In every case, you gain information from and make meaning of your feelings. And you become either imprisoned or liberated by your meaning-making.

Most of us have a large share of pleasant memories to fortify us through the rough ones. You may have noticed that your stronger feelings are associated with your most challenging, painful, or sorrowful experiences. It is possible that you have lived through horrors and traumas to which no one ought to be subjected. These memories can be hard to shake. They stay alive in us, giving rise to fresh painful feelings that may seem as real today as they were in the past. You may even believe that you are trapped in the trauma of that experience.

Some feelings that are too painful to acknowledge may remain under the surface of your awareness. In order to survive a horrific wrong, you may have dissociated from the experience and, in a fugue-like state, suppressed feelings related to your memories. When particularly painful memories begin to surface from the past, you may or may not feel ready or strong enough to acknowledge them. You may feel thrown by them, shaken by them rising to the surface of your mind. Memories, and the feelings connected to them, may sneak up on you, grabbing your attention. They grabbed Alicia's attention in the fall of 2017, when she fell into a deep depression.

Alicia had just returned from a week-long trip that left her so emotionally and physically drained that she spent the next month in bed in her parents' basement. She felt smothered in darkness and was consumed with anger because her mind and body were failing her once again. Suffering from physical pain and exhaustion, she napped most of the day and was awake most of the night, unnourished. Then, in the midst of her shutdown, two little words surfaced that brought back distressing memories she thought she had put behind her: "Me too."

The #metoo movement was in full swing in the media at this time and Alicia's memories of trauma were triggered by women and men posting painful, raw stories of abuse, or simply the words "me too." Although she was not ready to share her story, she found she could no longer ignore the ghosts of her past. Deeply depressed, she was overwhelmed with grief and horrified to realize that she had been suppressing her traumatic memories for so long. She finally resorted to treatment and medication. Adjusting to the medication was rough. It made her zombie-like and practically mute, so it was more difficult than ever for her to socialize. This was all happening in the weeks before her brother's wedding and she felt dissociated, exhausted, and unable to participate fully in all the celebrations.

Throughout years of therapy, Alicia never assumed the label of victim. But now she has come to realize that this insistence on her own personal power resulted in the worst kind of metaphysical malpractice—an assumption that she had been complicit in her abuse. Alicia has begun to share bits and pieces of her memories, and more of her feelings are surfacing. She is in the process of forgiving the people involved and trying to release her previously repressed anger. She sees now that she justified the abuses more than she ever vilified the perpetrators. It has been a pivotal shift for her to accept that what happened to her was not okay, but she has chosen to prioritize her reconciliation with herself. At those times when she needs to be reminded of her power, she visualizes walking alongside herself as the child and young adult who experienced that pain and needed to feel safe. In this way, she honors both her memories and her feelings.

When Linda learned of her daughter's past trauma, she was thrown into an abyss of gut-wrenching helplessness and sorrow. Although Alicia's guardedness through the years had made Linda uneasy, she could never penetrate it without becoming intrusive. She felt the full force of a dawning realization that she could not keep her children safe or alleviate their suffering. She wept.

We are often encouraged by our culture to ignore or suppress our feelings. We are constantly corrected for what are seen as socially unacceptable outbursts when we are children, and are schooled in what is proper to do and say. All of this conditions us to hide our feelings. But the cost of suppressing emotions may be a gradual inability to recognize your feelings or a tendancy to distrust them as if they were harmful or bad.

Linda grew up in a home where her parents were uncomfortable with displays of emotion. As a child, she frequently got in trouble for expressing her feelings. When she was giddy with happiness, her father warned her: "After laughing comes crying." It was never okay to express anger, and crying was treated merely as drama. As a teenager, she often cried in sheer frustration when trying to communicate her feelings to her parents. Then, at age twenty-one, she moved into a yoga community, where she opened up to her emotional life.

Linda quickly settled into the daily routines and disciplines of ashram life. At evening *satsang*, she joined the hundred or so others sitting cross-legged on floor pillows who seemed capable of freely expressing their feelings, finding it strange that no one stopped them or reprimanded them. In fact, no one appeared to think these displays inappropriate at all. Then one night, she found herself utterly unable to control her emotions during satsang. She alternated between hysterical laughter and heart-wrenching sobs. And no one stopped her. No one interfered in any way with the purity of her experience. She felt completely free.

If you are healing from past trauma, proceed gently and with professional support where needed. Congratulate yourself every time you uncover fresh feelings and integrate them. Begin to honor your feelings, allowing them in rather than suppressing them. If you have been suppressing or denying your feelings, it may be challenging for you to trust yourself to survive them. If that is the case for you, try permitting yourself safe emotions, in safe settings. Practice with common everyday feelings like pleasure, pain, frustration, and optimism.

If you have ever been the victim of overwhelming trauma, know that whatever happened to you can never eradicate or diminish the *you* of you, the *you* that existed long before you were forced to suffer pain, perhaps by people you trusted. The *you* that persists—the *you* that is innocent, optimistic, thoughtful, empathic, and powerful—is the *real* you. As Linda told Alicia: "The real you is there underneath everything, independent of your harrowing memories, speaking out in a voice of strength and courage."

Affirmation to Honor Feelings

I believe in a benevolent universe
Where it is safe for me to feel what I feel.
I never need fear my feelings,
For my feelings are messengers.
They reveal to me what I know is important
But what I have been hesitant to admit.
I allow my feelings, knowing they come and go,
Naturally, fleetingly.
They are unreasonable. I cannot control them
Or time them appropriately.
But I need not be afraid of my feelings.
By means of them, I come to know myself,
My whole, magnificent self.
Feelings, I respect you.

HONOR YOUR NEEDS

Healing requires exquisite self-care, radical self-determination, and the cultivation of community. When you honor and attune to the needs of your body, mind, and spirit, you prepare the way for dramatic healing breakthroughs. Alicia found a way to change her self-perceived weaknesses and turn them into self-actualized strengths in a book called *The Empath's Survival Guide* by Dr. Judith Orloff. After reading it, she felt reborn. In its pages, she found self-validation and a true sense of peace.

Throughout her childhood and young adulthood, Alicia had unknowingly attempted to cope with an empathic nature that she believed was a curse rather than a gift. Trying to protect herself from the vibrations and feelings of others, she developed eating disorders, addictions, and some interesting compulsions, like color-coordinating her meals and counting on her fingers as she sang the ABCs to make sure the alphabet really contained twenty-six letters. But Orloff's book positioned her for remarkable healing. When she came to understand herself as an empath, she became stronger and more balanced. This strength and balance made her more able to set firm boundaries and prioritize her own well-being over her tendency to be a compulsive people-pleaser. She learned to pay attention to her own vital energy in public settings and to leave them when necessary. The quality of Alicia's relationships improved as she came to know herself as an empath. She has developed the capacity to care for and about others without taking on their concerns, which has allowed her to be more present in her own life.

One of the greatest challenges for an empath is to maintain healthy boundaries. Empaths try to remain available to handle everyone else's crises and emotional disturbances, all the while ignoring their own. The key is to become intentional with the time you spend responding to others, because making the choice to engage can pull you out of seclusion—for better or for worse. Don't ignore your friends. Just make sure that you are prepared to listen without taking on their stories. We all need to respect and protect ourselves first. It is perfectly okay to "unplug," as long as you recognize that you are doing it by choice, not merely to avoid.

Our culture shifts back and forth between two extremes. On the one hand, we regard self-sacrifice as a virtue and tend to see honoring our own needs as selfish. Obituaries are full of praise for people who would do anything for anybody, gladly give the shirt off their backs, and put everyone else's needs ahead of their own. At the same time, self-care has become associated with hyperconsumerism and overindulgence. Of course, being helpful to others and caring about them is praiseworthy. But a compulsive need to take care of others at our own expense is not. So go ahead and schedule a massage or buy a new outfit; just remember you cannot buy your way to well-being.

Well-being is a practice. The growing trend of minimalism teaches that the need for more is almost always a sign that you need less. Doing what you need to do for your own well-being, however—whether or not it is endorsed by others, whether or not you get praised for it—positions you for healing. Exquisite self-care starts with honoring your needs and incorporating the activities and practices that fit with your lifestyle practices that nourish and stir your soul yet require little effort. Alicia has found, for instance, that while depression sometimes drives her need for isolation, there are many times when that solitude feels restorative and provides a much-needed retreat. Understanding this has encouraged her to become the self-proclaimed queen of self-care and naps.

It is gutsy to stand by your decisions, without wavering in the face of others' judgment. It takes courage to stand in the line of fire. This is what we call "radical self-determination"—a persistent commitment to live in authenticity and make choices that validate the true you. You are your own governing body, and radical self-determination is your personal proclamation that nothing and no one can inhibit your power of intention.

You don't need to say "yes" to every invitation if you are feeling the need for rest and recovery. You don't need to apologize for cancelling plans when you need time to yourself. Just make sure you are intentional about the plans you make. If you make a date with a friend, look forward to your time together; truly *choose* to be there. And most important, learn to make peace with your decisions.

Honoring your needs also consists of finding your tribe. We need others. We need community. We acquire built-in communities in the form of our families, our co-workers, or other groups we associate with, but these are not automatically helpful to our healing. We need to be intentional and cultivate the relationships we choose.

When Alicia was diagnosed with Lupus, she found others' expressions of concern were not helpful—"You look like you are feeling better" or "I know someone who has Lupus who is doing great." But Lupus is an invisible disease and she had a hard time believing that others really understood what she was going through. So she joined a support group for people with chronic illnesses and disabilities so she could socialize and build a community with others whose experiences were similar to her own. They met once a month and shared their stories and struggles. This made her feel seen and heard in a way she had not even realized she needed. To hear other women talking about bizarre symptoms, relation-ship struggles, and loss of identity made her feel less isolated. But the real value of this group didn't lie in the honest sharing of experiences. It lay rather in the shar-ing of resources and supportive strategies. The members respected each other's circumstances and understood that each experience was unique. As they learned how others had successfully navigated through difficulties, they inspired one another.

Alicia also found a chosen community among her coworkers. The culture of her workplace was to lead with compassion, honesty, and patience in all situations. Although their jobs were stressful, they supported each other, sometimes laughing their way through the day. She kept a framed quote above her desk that read: "Always believe that something wonderful is about to happen." At least twice a day, she could be heard shouting out "Christmas Miracles!" to mark the tiniest of victories, and others picked up the habit. They did this for each other because they were a team.

Being part of a supportive community that truly honors your needs is critical for healing and maintaining wholeness. If you feel a longing for supportive community, but are unsure how to find one, create one. You are not alone. Someone else in your vicinity is also seeking support.

Affirmation to Honor Needs

Unapologetically, authentically,
I take good care of myself.
I am the one who determines
What I will have and not have,

What I will do and not do,
And how I will live.
I gather around me people who get me.
Supporting myself,
Being supported by my people,
I heal and I thrive.

HONOR YOUR ABILITY
TO WAIT

When we feel caught in limbo, in a state of incompletion or ignorance, it is easy to believe that something is missing, something is wrong, something is broken. But when we become too eager to get past this state, to bypass the discomfort it engenders in us, we risk losing its gifts.

In her early teens, Linda wrote poetry to work out unhappy feelings, uncertainties, and frustrations. When she began a poem on a rant, she invariably turned herself around and became intent on hopefulness and confidence. This is an example of the inner urge toward resolution that we all share. We all prefer the known to the unknown; we like to see where we are going, to see the road ahead. We'd rather reach conclusions than prolong questions. We prefer the comfort of certainty to the discomfort of uncertainty.

On the other hand, most of us can point to long stretches of coping with the unknown that were high points in our lives—times when we needed to stay in the question, remain openhearted, and feel our way forward. We recognize these as high points precisely because there were no ready answers. Anything was possible, and we were curious if not eager to discover a way ahead. There is great value in the unknown, when anything is possible. But when anything is possible, we mustn't hurry it. We must wait.

Waiting is staying where you are, delaying action until some future time, and this can be uncomfortable. We have been given mixed messages about waiting. On the one hand, we are told that patience is a virtue, that all good comes to those who wait, that anything worth having is worth waiting for. Wait. Just wait. Wait your turn. Wait for the weather to improve. Wait for your sweetheart to change her mind. Wait for the big day to arrive. Wait for the sun to shine, for the pain to subside. Wait with bated breath. Hurry up and wait. Wait for it! On the other hand, we are encouraged not to wait, to just do it, to get on with it. What are you waiting for?

Waiting can be troublesome. But can it also be valuable? Much of the problem with waiting comes from embedded theology—broad beliefs we have internalized from our religious upbringing and the wider culture. For instance: God doesn't give you more than you can handle. Consider the implications of this belief. It presumes there is a deity who imposes circumstances we must endure—as hardships or as a test of endurance. But are these unexamined beliefs true or are they just something we say to soothe the sufferer? As we wait for relief, we are told it will all unfold in God's time. God is in charge. God knows. It must be God's will.

Implicit in these messages is the Judeo-Christian understanding of a God who punishes and rewards. You must wait for God or be damned. But your waiting will be rewarded, like a child promised ice cream for behaving. Yet whether we believe that God is a deity or infinite creativity, we have to look upon our waiting in a more constructive way. Maybe waiting can be meaningful and useful.

To wait need not mean to be powerless. It can mean to hold on, to have patience, and to remain still. To wait can mean to look forward, to anticipate, to get ready. Both meanings have value. They are polarities with equal value that can help us through times of uncertainty. In many of the practices described in this book, you will find seemingly contradictory instructions: stop and go; pause and proceed; rest and act. Each of these opposites offers insight and each is helpful in turn. Stopping, pausing, or resting removes distractions and influences so that you gain breathing room. As a cup of broth allowed to sit untouched becomes clear when particles fall to the bottom, mental stillness can lead to clarity in which a formerly cluttered brain can notice fresh possibilities.

"Patience," Joyce Mercer tells us, "is not simply the ability to wait. It's how we behave while we're waiting." We can cultivate this behavior by spiritual practices that quiet the mind (see chapter 5). When we are patient, we suspend an exclusively human view of life and rise in awareness to the state of wholeness. In the state of wholeness, we are more than human, more than our circumstances. We are connected to universal wholeness, free from the bonds of our own concerns and able to be still, calm, and trusting.

Waiting encourages us to look forward, to anticipate, to get ready. Instead of scurrying to do something or go somewhere in desperation, waiting engages us in a mental exercise of positive anticipation that develops our capacity for creativity or imagination. It gives us the power to imagine success and fulfillment. Waiting is not a passive state of being that puts our lives on hold. Rather it is a time of preparation for what comes next. All that time we spend waiting for God to act, or waiting for a sign, or waiting against hope, could be spent getting ready, cultivating a consciousness in which we can accept the good we desire.

Hebrew scripture speaks of waiting on God or waiting for God using words like "hope," "expect," and "trust." In other words, it enjoins us to wait expectantly. None of these phrases imply a deity who acts to withhold the good. The Bible speaks of evil as something "unripe." To be evil, in this sense, is to be unready, out of step with your dreams. Think about waiting as a time of ripening— a time of coming to fruition. "All things are ready," Shakespeare claims, "if our mind be so." To wait is to get ready, to ripen.

Your ability to wait is an aspect of your spiritual power, your capacity for self-mastery. Choosing the way you wait is one way you demonstrate that power. By exercising self-mastery, you gain self-confidence as a whole being. You harness the power of your mind and the strengths of your spirit in service to the fullness of life. You heal any sense of something being missing, wrong, or broken. You accept the reality of wholeness as your natural state of being. You learn to ignore momentary setbacks and understand that healing is not a one-time occurrence, but rather living in a way that reconciles your human and spiritual identities.

Louise Hay challenges us to "claim and consciously use" this power. "We think so often that we are helpless, but we're not. We always have the power of our minds."

Affirmation to Honor Your Waiting

I am not thwarted by hysterical imaginings.
I am a deliberate creator.
I master my ability to wait gracefully while
At the edge of my seat in positive expectancy.
My twin capacities of stillness and action

Are not in conflict or competition.
I have room for each in turn.
I sense and respond to each in turn.
I sit with desire, remaining still.
I dance with desire, readying myself.
Waiting is not missing out, procrastinating,
 or settling;
Rather, waiting is my time
Devoted to wondrous, desirable possibilities.

CHAPTER 7

Reinforce Your Wholeness

There is a vitality, a life force, an energy, a quickening, that is translated through you into action, and because there is only one of you in all time, this expression is unique.

—Martha Graham, from *The Life and Work of Martha Graham*

Healing is an intentional, continual practice of choosing to live fully in every circumstance, in recognition of your innate wholeness. Wholeness is not something you achieve; it is something you realize as you navigate through challenging times. To do this, you must learn to assert your power, celebrate your prosperity, recognize your worth, heal your relationships, and manage

your pain. Below are some simple approaches for you
to practice.

ASSERT YOUR POWER

"I can't help myself." "Everyone is telling me what I should
and should not do." "This doesn't feel right, but I don't
know what else to do." "I wish I were bold enough to tell
them I disagree." "I can't complain or I might lose my job."
"It's a dangerous world." "My condition is incurable." "I
know I should speak up, but I can't." "I should take better
care of myself, but my family needs me." "There's nothing
I can do about it."

If you've ever uttered one of these sentences, you
have felt the sting of powerlessness—a primal emotion
triggered by the dominant and most ancient human need
to survive. For human survival, you need health, well-
being, and self-determination. You need to belong in
community; you need others. When your own needs and
the needs of others appear to clash, you may feel paralyzed, unable to satisfy *any* needs. But when you continually sacrifice yourself in favor of others, even when you
believe that others have your best interests at heart, you
can begin to feel helpless and powerless.

But we are never powerless. When Linda's multiethnic family moved to a suburb of Omaha, it seemed
like a good choice for them, even though her husband
and children were clearly in the minority. The schools

were highly rated. The neighbors were friendly. The cost of living was reasonable and they were within easy driving distance of shops and services. But when she visited a hair salon nearby, she overheard the stylist say: "A black couple bought the house down the street. I guess they'll sell to whoever has the money." She suffered through the appointment, but on the way home, she cried. After agonizing over how to respond, Linda eventually called the stylist and told her about her experience. She explained that her husband and children were black, and suggested that not everyone felt comfortable with her bigotry.

When the stylist explained that she had lived all her life in this non-diverse community, Linda encouraged her to open her heart to the changes happening there. Whether or not her feedback made any difference to the stylist, she felt better for having spoken up in a considered, kind, intentional manner. As a white woman, privileged by virtue of her whiteness, Linda has often felt powerless in the face of the unconscious bigotry and racism to which her husband and children have been subjected. But in this instance, she was able to hold her head high, knowing that healing happens only when our thoughts, words, and actions flow from spiritual power.

Whether your feelings of powerlessness stem from your personal circumstances or from generalized anxiety over world conditions, it helps to know that these personal feelings of powerlessness are not yours alone; in other words, you may be feeling the collective consciousness of fear, which can amplify your own feelings exponentially. But you are always capable of attuning to the power within you—your spiritual power—and bringing it out in your thoughts, words, and actions.

Former first lady Michelle Obama said this of spiritual power: "When they go low, we go high." When gripped by powerlessness in the face of negative or hurtful behavior or circumstances, go high by attuning to your spiritual power, your rightful capacity for concentration on truth and on what is most important right now. Assert your self-mastery and your spiritual authority.

You do not have to fear helplessness. You can always claim your rightful spiritual power. When you act from spiritual power, you never say: "I can't." You say: "What can I do to improve this situation?"

Affirmation to Assert Power

When I feel paralyzed by powerlessness,
May I remember that spiritual power is natural
  to me.
May I attune to spiritual power in the atmosphere
  around me,
Internalizing it with every beat of my heart.
May the rhythm of my own heart be the drum
  of power
Fortifying me, egging me on.
May I dance to the beat, feel powerful in my body,

And may the words flowing from my lips be as
Respectful as they are true.

CELEBRATE YOUR PROSPERITY

Howard Hughes wanted more of everything. He wanted
more money, so he parlayed inherited wealth into a
billion-dollar empire. He wanted more fame, so he went
to Hollywood and became a filmmaker and star. He
wanted more sensual pleasures, so he paid handsome sums
to indulge his every hedonistic urge. He wanted more
thrills, so he designed, built, and piloted the fastest air-
craft in the world. He wanted more power, so he secretly
curried political favor with the power elite. All he ever
wanted was more. And yet Hughes ended his life living
in darkness, isolated from the rest of humanity, watching
old movies, and drinking soup. He died an impoverished
billionaire.

Howard Hughes is an extreme example, but he can
teach us a valuable lesson. When you hear yourself say,
"There's too little time," or "I don't have enough," or
"I'm on a fixed income," or "I can't afford it," or "There's
only a little left," these pronouncements are symptoms
of an inflammatory mental condition based on a belief
in scarcity.

A belief in scarcity means believing that there is never
enough—of food, of clothing, of pleasure, of just about
anything. This belief is fueled by a culture of instant

gratification and greed that makes scarcity appear to be a reality. At the root of this belief is the assumption that there are winners and losers, that there is only so much room at the top, that if someone else succeeds there won't be any left for you. Someone very close to us who was suffering from intractable clinical depression once remarked that she had no right to be happy as long as anyone else in the world was unhappy. But life is not a zero-sum game.

So how can we counter this belief that there is never enough and cultivate a consciousness of plenty? By giving and receiving. "The universe operates through dynamic exchange," Deepak Chopra assures us:

> Giving and receiving are different aspects of the flow of energy in the universe, and in our will-ingness to give that which we seek, we keep the abundance of the universe circulating in our lives.

You cannot help but notice, once you comprehend giving and receiving as a flow, that every time you perceive you are lacking—in affection, in friendships, in material possessions, in money—you are, in fact, hoarding or withholding this very thing. Every time. The remedy, in every case, is to start *giving* what you feel you lack. When Linda wanted more affection from her husband, she discovered that she had withdrawn hers. When she determinedly increased her expressions of affection, it worked like magic.

Want more friends? Become a good friend. Want more stuff? Clear out and give away unused belongings in your garage, your closets, your drawers. Want more money? Give some to your church or a charitable cause; or pay for someone's coffee.

As you give, so you receive. Receiving takes care of itself, for when you give generously, lavishly, you receive the satisfaction that cures the belief in scarcity. You indeed experience greater peace, health, and plenty. As Catherine Ponder reminds us: "You are prosperous to the degree you are experiencing peace, health, and plenty in your world."

Affirmation to Celebrate Prosperity

My eyes that can perceive lack and limitation
Are also able to see plenty and possibility.
I bravely and boldly know that I am divine,
Fully able to prosper by looking for reasons
    to celebrate
And appreciate the good that I can see.
I choose to live in assurance of ever-flowing,
Never-depleting abundance.
May I know that all the good I desire is
Right where I am, in my next breath.

By the power of plenty,
I peacefully and passionately pursue my dreams.
Let there be plenty for me to give in a spirit of
    generosity.
Let me receive graciously, gratefully.
All that flows from me and to me is a gift and a
    blessing.

RECOGNIZE YOUR WORTH

After a year of Sundays volunteering in youth ministry, Alicia was amazed that the lessons she set out to teach had been taught to her a thousand times over by her students. After explaining abundance as "having a bunch of something," she asked her students: "What is something you would like more of in your life?" She expected the children to respond with material possessions like clothes or toys. Instead, she received answers like "friendship," and "love," and "connections," and "relationships," and "emotions." The thoughtful responses she received prompted her to put the question to herself in a different way: "What do I want to *be* more of in this life?"

Have you talked to a toddler lately? They seem to have mastered the art of abundance. They are apt to tell you that they have a whole bunch of something when really it is more likely a small amount. Abundance feels that way. It is that exaggerated, blessed state of being that leads you to say: "I have a bunch of something!"

When we attribute who we are to our abundance, we take ownership—whether it's helpful or not! The easiest examples of this are kindness and sickness. No one wants to affirm: "I am in the state of being sick." Say it out loud; it sounds wrong. Most of us, however, would love to affirm: "I am in the act of being kind." That not only sounds right; it feels good. In fact, we tend to measure our own success and worth by the things we have and do, rather than the things we are. Our being, or our state of being, seems to hold no merit. But shouldn't it? When someone says, "Tell me about yourself," we tend to respond with a typical laundry list of our roles in society and our accomplishments. But when we are asked to describe someone else, we tend to answer with what they embody and what we see in them. And this is the truly important stuff!

So when someone asks you to describe yourself, ask yourself first what you want to *be* more of in this life. Let your state of being define you. Describe yourself in affirmative "I am" statements that feel right to you. Own the experiences and opportunities that you are passionate about and honor the goals you are trying to achieve. Own what you *are* and live in a state of abundance. Let adjectives become your accolades! "You either walk into your story and own your truth," Brené Brown warns, "or you live outside of your story, hustling for your worthiness."

As a child, Linda loved to sit on a beach just at the water's edge, where spent waves lapped the land and each receding wave deposited an accumulation of ocean refuse around her—lengths of seaweed and shards of shells. She was fascinated by the diverse designs of the tiny half shells, each of which held a minuscule life that had contributed to the well-being of its environment. Small as they were, each held myriad grains of sand you could count for a lifetime and never reach the end. This is abundance. When you feel small in relation to the world around you and question whether you can make a difference, consider the abundance that Linda discovered. Recognize that your living, your participating at any moment wherever you are, fulfills your purpose for being. A microscopic grain of sand in a tiny seashell can contribute to the vitality and beauty of the shore. Surely you can never be too small to make a difference.

Mrs. M was a peanut-sized spitfire with a supersized spirit. Born during the Roaring Twenties when most roads were unpaved, when home entertainment meant gathering around the radio, and when air conditioning meant opening windows and doors, she lived her life in loving devotion to her large family, unselfishly caring for their daily needs and always making room for others around her kitchen table. Everyone who dropped in there was welcome to enjoy her home cooking, all spiced with her special secret ingredient—love.

Simply put, Mrs. M was abundant in love. When you entered the room, she treated you as if you were the *only* person, greeting you with a smile of delight that said you were welcome and important. You could spend countless hours sitting in her kitchen being relieved of your burdens as, with a twinkle in her eye, Mrs. M calmed you, supported you, and encouraged you with words like: "Don't be afraid." "Life is beautiful." "Go live your life." "Be happy." "Come back and tell me all about it." Mrs. M never won any awards. She didn't make a big splash in the world beyond her own family and friends. But, in her own arena, in her own home, Mrs. M demonstrated abundance each day, giving where and how she could to everyone around her. May you, like Mrs. M, believe—and act as if—you are enough.

When Alicia started performing, she quickly learned that auditioning was just another way to squelch her self-confidence. She tortured herself with her need to be overprepared and perfect, then often crumbled at the actual audition—at least by her standards. On one of her first tours, a director sat the cast down and told them one by one what he saw in them and what he was getting from them as performers. In Alicia, he said, he saw a story of delayed gratification, pointing out that she was often overlooked because she was quiet and held back. His eyes sparkled as he said he was excited to see what she would do when she stepped forward and claimed her talent.

Those words really hit home for Alicia. They helped her become aware that she had to claim her own self-worth and counteract the insecurities she had carried from childhood. In her mostly white world, she was often confined to roles that were dictated by racial bias. When she did finally get the opportunity to play a lead role—Maria in *West Side Story*—she wondered whether it was based on her talent or on the fact that she looked the part. Looking back, she can now see that her own insecurities may well have been a factor in her delayed gratification. In many ways, she gave others an excuse to agree with her own fear that she was "not ready" or "not enough." But when she finally owned her talent and convinced herself that she was ready and knew her worth, you better believe they saw her. She earned her seat at the table.

The next time you fear that you are not enough, have the strength of mind to recognize the contribution you make, however insignificant you may judge it to be. Own your worth.

Affirmation to Recognize Your Worth

Centered in my awareness of an infinite source and
   universal mind,
I breathe and know I am enough.
I am enough of power, wisdom, and strength.
I am enough of understanding, order, will, and
   release.
I am enough of faith, zeal, imagination, and life.

Although I am not all of God or source or mind, all
   at once,
I am enough of that infinity, enough for this
   moment of need and realization.
Whenever my personal memories give me the
   false impression of not being enough,
I deliberately turn from my past and claim my
   divine identity.
Whenever I interpret the words or actions of
   another as a judgment of my inferiority,
I choose to disclaim my errant thoughts in favor of
   the truth that I am enough.
Whenever I experience a failure, setback, or
   disappointment,
I remind myself that I am courageous enough to
   strive for fulfillment.
I affirm my strength of character to know
That every circumstance and every experience
   appear for love.
Love is the great magnet of the universe,
My calling to be unified and whole in every
   experience
Whether labeled good or bad.
I am enough of divine love for everything and
   everyone I encounter
Every day.
I am!

HEAL YOUR RELATIONSHIPS

Belonging is a basic human need. We need others. Within relationships, we have a chance to see ourselves more clearly and behave more compassionately than we ever could in isolation. Whenever you feel out of sorts in a significant relationship, you are out of sorts with yourself. To heal your relationship, you must heal your own mind and heart. You can do this by following three simple recommendations: don't rush to conclusions, always set reasonable expectations, and never criticize or condemn. "If you want others to be happy," the Dalai Lama teaches, "practice compassion. If you want to be happy, practice compassion."

Don't Rush to Conclusions

When we rush to conclusions, we tend to misinterpret or prejudge others. Learn instead to respect others enough to ask for an explanation or clarification. Consider the woman whose seventy-year-old neighbor regularly climbed on his riding mower early in the morning and proceeded noisily back and forth across his lawn, destroying her attempts at meditation. "Why can't that idiot wait 'til later to do this?" she grumbled. Only long after her non-loving response did she learn that his wife was dying in hospice care, so he tended the lawn early so he could be with her all day. Or consider the man who braved the ice, sleet, and snow to meet a friend at a café for lunch.

He waited for thirty minutes, but she never showed up. "Typical," he fumed. "She's so spacey. Always late." But when he returned to his office, he found a message saying his friend was still waiting for him at another café—the one where they had originally agreed to meet. He had forgotten to write it on his calendar.

It's these little things, these small judgments and momentary unkind thoughts, that add up, over time, to disharmony in relationships. They accumulate along the way. But there are big things, as well, that impact relationships. And the way you manage the little things can make a huge difference in how you respond when the big ones arise. Who have you been practicing *being?* That's what matters in all cases.

Set Reasonable Expectations

We have an unfortunate tendency to expect others to be everything to us—to fulfill us. Learn instead to allow others to be self-determining and independent, just as you wish to be. Consider the television series that begins with the husbands of two seventy-year-old women announcing they are divorcing their wives in order to marry each other. All four characters have to adjust to changing conditions. Each has to deal with shattered expectations and the inability to control the others. They leap between extremes of feelings and behaviors, one moment throwing stinging indictments—"You never cared about me!"—

the next, extending compassion. When one character, frightened during an earthquake, hides under a table, her ex-husband leaves his soon-to-be-husband at home to join her and hold her hand. As their stories unfold, each character grapples with his or her entrenched ideas of marriage and friendship. Each one questions their own past and present choices, and each one becomes more self-defining and self-determining.

Reconcile, Don't Condemn

Our tendency to condemn rather than reconcile, to reject rather than accept, can derail our own attempts at healing. We must seek to understand and harmonize, to be humble and noble, rather than putting forth negative thoughts and criticism. In one episode of a popular British series, a woman whose husband adored her appeared terrified to have him near when she went into labor. When the baby was born, it became clear why. Although she and her husband were both white, the newborn had obvious African traits. Everyone hushed in suspense as the husband approached his wife's bed and saw the infant for the first time. After a seeming eternity of stunned silence, he reached for the child and, in a remarkable example of the spiritual power of understanding, whispered: "My beautiful boy." The husband decided who he would be, choosing holy reconciliation and the harmony of love.

To forgive the seemingly unforgivable is possible only when we humbly recognize that all of us are capable of helpful as well as harmful behavior. We honor those who model for us the capacity to forgive those who have wronged us. But it is just as important for wisdom to partner with love. What some see as "tough love," we see as wisdom and love working together. An episode of a popular medical series portrays a doctor and her husband, an FBI agent who had relapsed into a gambling addiction, renegotiating their relationship. She insisted that he leave their home, knowing that she needed to stand strong and not enable his addiction. Despite his pleas to return, she remained adamant, telling him it was too soon. But as she walked away, she turned and softly said: "I love you."

Affirmation to Heal Relationships

No matter what was said or done,
No matter my imaginings,
Let me see through a filter of love
Your innocence. Your humanity.
Let me translate love into kindness,
Compassion, mercy, and grace.
When I look at you, let me see myself.
The words that I speak?
Let them be encouraging words.
The actions that I take?
Let them be caring as well as clear.

My open heart and open mind
Together in love and wisdom
Walk my way back to you
And home to myself.

MANAGE YOUR PAIN

Pain is a particular feeling that is subjective and generally difficult to describe. Pain consumes our attention,
that's why we say that it "grabs" us or "gnaws" at us. Pain
is both a mental and a biological phenomenon. It stems
from an emotion arising within your brain as a response
to an acute physical injury, a chronic physical condition,
or debilitating feelings about your circumstances. But,
no matter how you define it or what you believe causes
it, pain is real. It is never all in your head. In fact, pain
comes from a complex interaction among body parts and
body systems, interpreted by the brain and manifested as
a physical sensation or an inability to manage in particular ways.

Physical pain is easier to name and locate, and easier
for others to comprehend. Mental pain can be difficult to
describe, leading the sufferer as well as others to suspect
it is unreal. Mental pain, however, is real pain! Although
it may be described in emotional terms—perhaps as
anxiety, depression, hopelessness, or rage—mental pain
can have real physiological effects, like a racing heart, or
digestive distress, or joint inflammation, or exhaustion.

Pain is not meant to be ignored. Pay attention to it. Do what you need to do to take good care of yourself. In addition to whatever other techniques you use for pain reduction, try one or more of the practices we recommend in chapter 5. And above all, do not be afraid to feel your pain.

The trick is to learn to lean into your pain. Alicia has come to appreciate the effectiveness of this through a technique used by her massage therapist. When she identifies a point of gripping pain, she relaxes and the therapist presses her elbow on the spot, holding steady until the pain subsides and all that is left is the pressure of her elbow. This physical technique can also be adapted for leaning into uncomfortable situations, feelings, and conditions. Just put gentle spiritual pressure on them to help them peacefully exit the stage.

You have to be willing to acknowledge pain's presence in your life, because it rarely gives you a chance to ignore it. In some ways, pain is like the old concert T-shirt that hasn't fit you for years, but that still takes up space in your dresser drawer. It is there as a constant reminder of who you have been, but does not reflect all that you have gained.

In *The Life-Changing Magic of Tidying Up*, Marie Kondo puts great emphasis on thanking the uncomfortable conditions and feelings you are ready to release. We all look for valuable lessons in the rough spots we have gone through when we look back on them. But when you are right in the thick of these situations, it may seem difficult or inauthentic to thank your pain. Instead, try expressing gratitude for the space you are actively creating in order to heal.

Affirmation to Manage Pain

I turn my attention toward the center of my being,
Where the power of love lives deep within.
I breathe deeply, in a state of divine love,
The love that casts out fear, eases tension,
And brings peace.
With every heartbeat divine life pulses,
Bringing relief and release to every point of pain.
With every breath wholeness radiates within,
And each cell vibrates with the fullness of life.
I rest with ease in my true state of wholeness,
Peace, and well-being.

—Adapted from *Silent Unity*

CHAPTER 8

Share Your Story, Inspire Others

The vision that you glorify in your mind, the ideal
that you enthrone in your heart, this you will build
your life by, this you will become.

—James Allen, *As a Man Thinketh*

We all have a story to share. The stories you share of your
courage and conviction, your resilience and optimism,
your resourcefulness and creativity, will inspire others.
Moreover, as you share your story, you reinforce it. You
inspire yourself! So every day, live fully and tell the story
of your wholeness.

We have drawn inspiration from many people who
graciously and courageously shared their stories with us

about healing and recovering their innate knowledge of wholeness. Here are three that we hope will inspire you as you claim your own wholeness.

GARY

Gary awoke with numb feet. When he found he could not walk it off, he underwent medical tests, first for diabetes and then for neurological abnormalities. When a nurse called to schedule a follow-up appointment, citing "evidence of demyelination," he asked her to say that in English. She replied: "You have multiple sclerosis."

More tests followed, including a spinal tap. Medicine given to alleviate the primary symptom of numb feet made no appreciable difference. Over time, other symptoms appeared, including one known as an MS band, an unusual, uncomfortable tightening around the midsection. Steroids were prescribed.

Gary had worked his way through college, earning a master's degree in public administration, then started his career as a presidential management intern in Washington, DC, performing cost-benefit studies and policy/program analyses. Eventually, however, he and his wife, Sue, decided to return to Texas to raise their family. At the time of his diagnosis, he had been working for two years as a consultant with a small private company in Dallas. Life was good, their toddler son was thriving, and he loved his work, which seemed tailor-made for his skills and talents.

Gary was managing MS well, but when their second son arrived, he really began to notice the effect that fatigue was having on him. Travel and other tasks that had formerly been energizing became exhausting, although he did his best to hide it. Specialists prescribed one medication after another, but none of them helped. His symptoms drove him deeper and deeper into depression, and he eventually ended up in the hospital, where he remained for a week.

Seven years after his diagnosis, Gary accepted a new job in his hometown of San Antonio, and his family settled into a new home, full of enthusiasm. But unpredictable symptoms began to flare and then subside, and, within two years, it became apparent that Gary's health would have to become his priority. When he began to recognize that tasks he had performed with great proficiency and ease for so long were becoming all but impossible, he knew something was seriously wrong. An MRI revealed significant changes in his brain, showing that his cognitive abilities—particularly those related to executive function and others that were critical to his work—had declined and would continue to decline. To encourage him, his doctor emphasized that Gary would still be *Gary*. He would not lose his identity. With this small consolation, Gary applied for disability and eventually left his job, having been told that the odds of his returning to work were zero. This news stopped him in his tracks. Sixty days earlier, he had signed a new home mortgage. He was forty-three years old.

"Throughout my adult life," Gary recalls, "work had made up a large part of my identity. I had worked hard to succeed in my profession and was used to being busy, productive, and responsible. Now I had to ask myself what I would do with the sixty hours each week that I had devoted to meaningful work. How would I be able to provide for my family without a job?"

Gary was beset by questions about healing. "What is the nature of healing and how can I heal in the face of a condition that medical professionals have verified is ravaging the life of my dreams?" "How is healing possible when the disease is a fact that I must deal with daily for the rest of my life?" "How do I heal when the word 'incurable' has been whispered in my ear?" "If I can no longer think and act as I used to, then who am I? And if I am not myself—if I do not recognize myself—what good can healing do?" He began to believe that the universe was against him and he railed against his condition. "I do not deserve to have my body working against me." "I do not deserve to be deprived of professional fulfillment." "I do not deserve to be stopped in the prime of life." He believed his life was over.

But then he realized that his life wasn't over, and that nothing was against him.

         This Life Is Yours

"Healing began when I heard a message that changed my relationship with myself," Gary remembers. "The message? 'You are a divine being. Your identity is greater than only-human.' Until I internalized this message, I didn't think I deserved anything better. I didn't love myself enough to heal. I had to learn see myself in a different way—as capable rather than incapable; as strong rather than helpless; as worthy rather than unworthy. It was a huge step," he admits. "Enormous. When I began to value myself, everything looked different in the light of this new understanding."

Some conditions are visible; no one has to ask you about them. Other conditions, like MS, are not, so people don't easily understand them. When people told Gary, "Man, I wish I didn't have to work," comments like this triggered deep insecurity and feelings of failure. Yet, every time he viewed his circumstances from the premise of his divine nature, Gary felt empowered, privileged even, to live the life he had. When he stopped comparing his life to the lives of others, he began to appreciate the time he now had to be present to his boys in ways that would not have been possible if he were working the hours he had in the past.

Financial challenges came along with MS, of course. Gary's family income was cut in half. Retirement went away. Sue took a job that paid 15 percent less and medical expenses more than doubled. For a former high achiever charged with providing for his family, having to rely on his wife in a totally new and unexpected way and living on a disability check instead of a paycheck cut to the core of Gary's ego. Time and again, he had to meditate his way to equanimity, surrendering his long-held construct of what it means to be a man.

Now, whenever Gary suffers an acute flare-up, he accepts it as a fresh opportunity to see his life in a context of wholeness. He has learned to manage the fear that comes with each exacerbation. "It's like post-traumatic stress," he says, "only it's freshly traumatic to worry that, this time, I could become permanently bedridden." On one occasion, when his oldest son was a freshman in high school, he felt extraordinarily tired and awoke from a nap to find that he couldn't walk. Using his upper body strength, he crawled downstairs. Two weeks, an ER visit, and a $35,000 injection later, his legs began to feel normal again. But living day to day with the unpredictability of MS has taught Gary to be grateful for small and simple successes. "If I can wiggle my toes, bend my knees, and lift my body out of bed," he claims, "I see it as a miracle. I have learned that I am divine and that these moments of particular ability are a gift."

Gary has learned to manage his symptoms with doses of good humor, often breaking the tension with self-deprecating comments. "Knowing I am a divine being," he says, "helps me see that my life is greater than my disease and that I have inner resources like spiritual strength, wisdom, and order that I can command." With all that has changed about his life, he has never lost his determination to participate in everything that he cares about—whether organizing an event for his son's high school band or joining a planning team at church. But he has also learned to respect and respond to his body's needs, honestly assessing what is and is not possible. And this has been one of the greatest struggles for him—to surrender to the needs of the day. "Saying 'no' has become a self-care practice rather than a sign of defeat," he observes. "I am learning to be at peace with what is. Peace is healing. Peace is working in cooperation with my life rather than against it."

Gary is thankful for the healing and the power of spiritual understanding that have come along with the realization that he is divine. He now enjoys a broad awareness that the universe is an atmosphere of benevolence—that it is not out to get him. "No deity is punishing me," he declares. "No external power is causing my condition. The relief I felt when I began to realize my divine nature is indescribable. It allowed me to let go of magical thinking and claim my inborn capacity of self-mastery—the knowledge that all the power I had assigned to God was flowing within me. I have the power to steer my thinking and my behavior, to insist that appreciation be my dominant attitude. Even on days when I choose poorly, I can choose again."

For Gary, every day is now a fresh opportunity to choose his perception, to view his life in its entirety, to see his own wholeness. "Every day I get to wrestle with thoughts and feelings that would tell me otherwise, that would reduce my view until I would see only broken parts. I call upon spiritual understanding every day, reminding myself that I am divine. It is my internal GPS."

KELLY

As a preteen, Kelly made a pact with her swim team to implement healthier eating. Everyone agreed to cut out a different type of junk food for each month that year. She dove in with gusto, never imagining that agreement would take on a life of its own. She began to restrict far more than junk food, and her restrictions became cumulative. She eliminated more and more over time. She thought she was on a diet just like everyone else, and that she just happened to be really good at it. It wasn't until she started purging that she knew she was in trouble.

By the age of twelve, Kelly had set her heart on an acting career. Her training as an actress, dancer, and singer required a lot of self-discipline, a skill she had already mastered. She felt energized with less food in her belly, so she consumed less—and purged more—convinced that being skinny would ensure her career success. She continued this pattern for years, right up until her first hospitalization for anorexia. At seventeen, she landed in a children's hospital and, at twenty-one, in residential treatment. During all this time, she never allowed herself to be in a committed relationship with recovery. "I fought with the staff rather than facing myself," she admits. "I got a thrill out of sneaking away to throw up; I fell into a pattern of self-harming."

When Kelly finally decided to get serious about recovery, she was forced into the fear and discomfort of facing herself. She accepted some of what she learned in treatment, but her mindset of resistance and denial only prolonged her recovery. "I left treatment thinking that I was well if I ate only *healthy* foods," she remembers. "Then one day, when I was offered a gluten-free dairy-free cupcake, I burst into tears. It didn't matter that the cupcake was made from healthy ingredients, I knew I could not be the girl who ate the cupcake."

At twenty-six, Kelly started seeing a private therapist. It was then that recovery began to feel possible. "I lived alone," she explains, "so there was no one to hide things from. That was when I began to unravel the myth that eating disorders are about body image and realized that I had a genetic predisposition toward anorexia. I just felt calmer when I was starving, and starving myself helped me cope with my feelings of not being whole, not being 'enough.' I began to see the relationship between purging food and the need to purge the pain of traumatic memories. For me, genetics loaded the gun and life pulled the trigger. In fact, food actualized my fears."

The key for Kelly was to accept that she was accountable for her actions. The first time she ate out in public after therapy was a challenge, because she was confronted with a menu over which she had no control. "The friend who was meeting me for dinner was running a bit late," she recounts, "so I paced outside the restaurant singing to myself to avoid going inside and sitting at a table alone." But her friend did everything right when he arrived. He ordered the exact same meal she did and mirrored her pace as she ate so she wasn't left staring at a plate full of food after he had finished. "It felt like the longest meal of my life," she acknowledges proudly, "but I made it through."

Kelly took another positive step toward recovery when she retired from acting, recognizing that her love affair with the stage stemmed from her need for an emotional outlet. It had been a way to mask her shame and hurt behind a character or costume. "Once I faced this and began to process those feelings," she observes, "I moved beyond my need for acting, knowing that the culture of the theater reinforced my disordered thinking and kept me from trusting my natural instincts. Acting had become just another aspect of my life over which I had little control—an aspect in which I always yielded creative control to someone else, giving them the power to dictate who I should be." By thus asserting her own power—her innate capacity for self-mastery—she reclaimed her true identity.

Gradually, Kelly became more and more able to try new things. She learned that, when she refused to let her fears define her, she could become an active participant in the pleasures of life. She could decide for herself which had the greater value: avoiding a friend's dinner party because she couldn't control the menu, or enjoying the opportunity to connect with friends. "Once I reasserted my true self," she claims, "I was more able to recognize when my thinking was disordered. When well-meaning friends noticed I was gaining weight, I had to work with myself to accept that it was okay. Why wouldn't it be okay to put on weight? I *wanted* to be the girl who could eat the cupcake."

For seventeen years of her life, Kelly was chained to an eating disorder that kept her from experiencing a full life of her own choosing. Now, she is a holistic nutritionist who specializes in eating-disorder recovery. Her personal experience has shown her the need to shift from institutionalized treatment methods that were heavily focused on caloric intake to an understanding of emotions and their relationship to food. "Treatment has to be individualized," she points out. "It needs to be grounded in small steps toward self-mastery. My work with clients requires that I continually do my *own* work. If I am going to have my clients sit down and eat a Big Mac, then I can't be the one freaking out over the Big Mac. We eat it together. We challenge the fear-foods together by focusing on the value of recovery, not just on how awful and uncomfortable it feels to be staring down the burger."

Today, Kelly has turned her back on a life dominated by an eating disorder. She has arrived at a place where she can acknowledge her past experiences without being locked into them. She actively pursues ways to push beyond her fears. Where she used to shrink and hide behind characters and costumes, she now chooses a more expansive sense of self, which means she claims wholeness. After years of being carefully controlled and only attempting things that felt safe, she has become willing to be vulnerable and forthcoming in order to support others. Kelly has moved into self-mastery.

For Kelly, recovery and true healing came through an awareness that she had the power to choose—the power to shape and control her own life. Moreover, she knows that this work is never done. There will always be choices to make. "But I trust my instincts now," she affirms. "I have confidence in my ability to maintain healthy boundaries and recognize when I have to take a step back and challenge false beliefs. I know I must question rather than deny or ignore my fears. This awareness does not eliminate the risk," she knows. "But I am confident that I am resilient and recovered, and I feel the truth in that."

SUE

Sue follows the spiritual path of Buddhism, in which healing consists of dissolving delusions about the nature of reality, about the permanence of conditions, and about the fallacy of separation-consciousness. But her faith was sorely tested when her partner, Linnie, died. She and

Linnie had created a life filled with love. Together with Linnie's daughter, they had built a loving family. Their needs were met; they could do whatever they chose to do, seemingly without limit. They lived life to the fullest every day, on their own terms. They were connected energetically and vibrationally, in a way that seemed to exemplify the true nature of human love.

But that love was threatened when Linnie learned she had breast cancer. Lumpectomy led to radiation, which led to remission. They were ready to move on. They traveled to Venice, Florence, and Hawaii. They cruised to Alaska twice. Life was grand. After a few years, they enrolled in some prosperity courses at a local Unity church that introduced them to ideas and practices that would become poignantly relevant as time went on. These practices pointed them in the direction of *living*, of creating the life they wanted, and of choosing how to navigate cancer treatment.

"Linnie's second diagnosis came just as I was launching a new business," Sue recalls, "something I had dreamed of doing for a long time. When Linnie began experiencing distressing symptoms, we learned that her breast cancer had metastasized. Knowing where the diagnosis would most likely lead, we decided not to retreat from life, not to hide or isolate ourselves, but rather to *live*. We created an environment in which we *chose* our attitudes and actions. We *chose* how we responded to the unwanted circumstances with which we were confronted. It was, after all, a part of our spiritual practice, and we had the benefit of many teachings to guide us."

Linnie and Sue decided to thrive. Through highs and lows, through debilitating treatments and periods of calm, they lived as well as possible each day. But gradually, very gradually, Linnie began to slow down and they knew she was headed toward death. When they talked about this impending certainty, Linnie expressed her concerns about how Sue would cope after her death. Knowing the depth of their attachment, she had a hard time imagining how Sue would be able to let her go. The great Buddhist teachings that had sustained Sue over the years are, after all, theoretical until experienced, and Sue was aware of her resistance to them in the face of this challenge. But she determined not to run from them and committed to facing her delusions head on. "I was learning that we can fall apart without breaking," Sue explains.

Sue witnessed Linnie swiftly progressing through the phases of dying, overcome with concern at times that their attachment would prevent her from letting go. "I went into our backyard meditation cabin," she recalls, "where I connected with Linnie spiritually, talking to her and asking her to give me a sign when she was ready." Certain things became clear to Sue during this time, especially the knowledge that she could help Linnie prepare for dying. Many people are averse to dealing with the details of dying, as if talking about it and preparing for it somehow abets death. Others simply deny the reality of death approaching and want to avoid it as long as possible. But Linnie and Sue's belief in wholeness taught them that they should not miss out on living in the face of dying.

"We each moved toward healing in a different way," Sue remembers. "I envisioned Linnie as a five-month-old fetus readying for birth into eternity, introducing an element of poignant excitement into my own feelings of advancing and aching loss. Linnie gathered lifelong friends and family around her as part of her own healing. I responded by being generous rather than stingy about the time others spent with Linnie, knowing I had to make room for that healing—to open the doors wide to those important relationships." Linnie identified some urgent priorities, including a trip to the mountains to celebrate her mother's ninetieth birthday. As protective as Sue was of her fragile condition, she recognized that Linnie belonged to her family, to her tribe, and that they were all bound in a spiritual reality, one wholeness. As Linnie's family, they would be eternally connected with her.

Sue and Linnie knew before the doctors told them when medical interventions were no longer productive. It was time for Linnie to tell her eighteen-year-old daughter that she was dying, so Sue arranged for them to spend a few days in the mountains, leaving her alone to process the certainty that Linnie was in her final days. "When Linnie returned," she relates, "I gathered her nearest and dearest around her and she died in my arms. Linnie had carefully orchestrated these last moments to support her through her struggle to cope with the conflicting desires of wanting to remain—perhaps for me, and certainly for her daughter—and wanting to exhale into whatever comes next.

"Everyone who knew Linnie knew her as unassuming, private, and humble," Sue declares. "But she was also profoundly powerful and inspiring to others." This became evident when a standing-room-only crowd spilled out of a 200-seat sanctuary for Linnie's memorial celebration of life. "The Buddhist practice of nonattachment notwithstanding," Sue admits, "I cried as I had never cried in my life. Linnie and I had created the life we had always dreamed of, and now I knew I had to continue living that life. I hear her saying, *This is the day, enjoy it.*' Together we had created great energetic consciousness conditions, and now I benefit from these."

In her work, Sue encourages others to take risks, stay connected, and celebrate interdependence—all in a spirit of impermanence. "I had to let Linnie go," she acknowledges, "but her dying was not a failure. Who she was is who she remains. And I now know that I can fall apart without breaking."

This Life Is Yours

Affirmation for Today

This day is for me. The hours I will live through
today are for me.
The day is laid out ahead of me, a wild landscape,
a blank canvas.
The me that is more than me, the me that is pure
spirit
Imbued with all wisdom and love, sets the scene
and takes the stage today.
May every decision I will make today nurture well-
being.
Grateful that I can choose my outlook and attitude,
I tame the wilds and calm the storms.
I walk in wholeness and paint a portrait of my true
identity.
Today I will attend to the needs of my body with
particular care.
I will lovingly support myself with healthful choices.
I will choose inspiration as my guide for anything I
choose to do today.
I know that whatever I let in—by viewing it,
reading it,
Hearing it, or participating in it—affects me.
I want my mind and heart engaged in
Life-enhancing, meaning-making moments.
I choose to live deliberately today.

CONCLUSION

Even after all this time
The sun never says to the earth,
You owe me.
Look what happens with a love like that.
It lights the whole sky.

—Daniel Ladinsky, *The Gift*

We both bless you and celebrate you. We will always know that nothing about you can ever be missing, wrong, or broken. We know that wholeness is the truth about you and we are champions of your choice to live fully each day. Here are our closing messages for you.

Alicia

When my mom first suggested that we write this book together, I felt as if I would be sharing my experiences from a place in my life where great things were happening to me, within me, and for me. I had started a new job, my energy levels and productivity were high, and I felt resilient, steady, and whole in every sense of the word. Then I hit a rough patch that sent my autoimmune symptoms flaring for almost the remainder of the time we were writing. I was in constant pain and presenting flu-like symptoms so often that I was regularly missing two or three consecutive workdays. I just could not feel well. I was panicked by the thought that we wouldn't make our deadline and that I would let my mom down. And I didn't really know when the flare-up would end.

But I knew I had a real opportunity to approach this book in a *whole*, new way. See what I did there? I am living the message right now. This was not going to be a come-out-on-the-other-side story; it was going to be a true test of my story and, therefore, a heck of a lot more relatable. I nurtured my wholeness by focusing on what I could do and adapted the plan. I remembered the truth of who I am and acknowledged that, challenges aside, I could feel and know that someone reading this book needed this version of me. Do you feel as if you have been handed a surplus of lemons and don't have the energy to make the lemonade? Then you may relate to and be encouraged by my experiences.

Linda

While writing this book, Alicia and I both had to adjust our expectations. I had to accommodate my own habits to my daughter's contributions, her work flow, and her sense of direction. I chose to be patient with a process and flow different from my own. Through these adjustments, I grew in my ability to exercise compassion as I allowed Alicia her experience. I learned to refrain from rescuing when my mom-compulsions flared.

Alicia was not the only one of us to deal with healing matters while writing this book. Mine were more emotional than physical. I experienced a load of mom-compulsions as Alicia revealed stories I had not heard before. And I had to confront my own "non-sense," some of which you've read about in these pages. But the experience has made our relationship stronger and we are grateful for the strength of our shared message.

If you are someone's parent, caregiver, or friend, you may recognize the challenge of standing as witness for their experience while navigating your own feelings about their circumstances. May our message encourage and support you.

APPENDIX

Index of Affirmations

ABOUT THE AUTHORS

Winner of the 2011 Best Spiritual Author competition for her first book, *How to Pray without Talking to God*, **Linda Martella-Whitsett** is an inspiring, respected Unity minister and spiritual teacher. She is vice president of Unity Prayer Ministry, including the 24/7 worldwide *Silent Unity*.

Alicia Whitsett is a first-time author and a lifelong student of Unity teachings. She has a BA from the University of Texas of the Permian Basin

HAMPTON ROADS
PUBLISHING COMPANY

... for the evolving human spirit

Hampton Roads Publishing Company publishes books on a variety of subjects, including spirituality, health, and other related topics.

For a copy of our latest trade catalog, call (978) 465-0504 or visit our distributor's website at *www.redwheelweiser.com*. You can also sign up for our newsletter and special offers by going to *www.redwheelweiser.com/newsletter/*.